Concept of the Self in the Light of Jaina Philosophy

Deepa Baruah

CANADIAN
Academic Publishing

2015

Concept of the Self in the Light of Jaina Philosophy

Deepa Baruah

(M.A, M. Phil.)

CANADIAN

Academic Publishing

2015

Price : $27.86

First Edition : May, 2015

ISBN : 978-1-926488-26-4

ISBN Allotment Agency : Library and Archives Canada (Govt. of Canada)

Published & Printed by
Canadian Academic Publishing
81, Woodlot Crescent,
Etobicoke,
Toronto, Ontario, Canada.
Postal Code- M9W 6T3
Phone- +1 (647) 633 9712
http://www.canadapublish.com

ACKNOWLEDGEMENT

At the very outset, I express my deep sense of gratitude to my respected madam Dr. Mukta Biswas, professor and Head, Department of Sanskrit, Gauhati University, for suggesting me to choose the topic of the present book. I am really grateful to her for her able guidance, valuable informations and help that I received during my study period and also during of preparation of the present book.

I am very much grateful to my supervisor Dr. Sujata Purkayastha, Reader, Department of Sanskrit, Gauhati University, for her constant encouragement and valuable advices.

I shall be failing in my duties if I do not my gratitude to my father Lt. Deva Baruah whose memory is a great inspiration to me. My mother Smt. Kusum Baruah, my uncle, Sri Ghana Baruah, my younger sister Manashi Baruah helped and inspired me all throughout my studies. I am thankful to them.

I express my gratitude to the Librarian and staff of K.K. Handique Library, Gauhati University, and the librarian of the Seminar Library of Sanskrit Department for their sincere help in providing me with full library facilities.

Deepa Baruah

PREFACE

The concept of the self or atman occupies a significant position in the history of Indian philosophy. Almost all the systems of Indian philosophy give their views about this concept. The concept of the self-propounded by the Jainas has the scope of critical examination as it is different in many ways from other systems of thought .Hence; it is proposed to prepare a discussion for the proper understanding as this very valuable concept. The aim of the present dissertation is to examine the concept of jiva or the self held by the Jaina from a critical standpoint.

The present book has been divided into six chapters including the introduction. In the introductory chapter, the historical background of Jainism is discussed. The second chapter deals with Jaina metaphysics. The third chapter deals with the Jaina concept of the self. In this content we have tried to give a short account of the concept the self in Nyaya-Vaisesika, Samkhya-Yoga and Advaita Vedanta systems.The fifth chapter deals with criticism of the Jaina concept of self. Finally, some conclusions are drawn based on the discussions made in these chapters.

Deepa Baruah

CONTENTS

CHAPTER – I

INTRODUCTION

The literal meaning of the word Philosophy means knowledge of the wisdom which has been derived from Latin word *Philos* and *Sophiya*. Indian Philosophical system is based on nine divisions which are Sankhya, Yoga, Mimamsa, Nyaya, Vedanta, Vaisesika, Jaina, Buddha and Carvaka. And again those divisions have been sub-divided into Orthodox and heterodox thinking, one who believes the authority of *Veda* and another who denies the same.

Authority of Veda is denied by the Jaina philosophy, so it is regarded as the Nastika Philosophy along with Buddha and Carvaka Philosophy. But it has similarity with the orthodox system of Indian Philosophy regarding ultimate aim of life. The ultimate aim of the orthodox and Jaina system is to achieve liberation (*moksa*) from bondage caused by the influx of *karman* into the soul. Different *paths* or ways has been described by the philosophers to obtain liberation. To obtain liberation Jaina philosophy advocates three means which are known as right faith (*samyak-darsana*), right knowledge (*samayak-jnana*) and right conduct (*samyak-caritra*).

Jainism is one of the oldest religions in India having its dogma, metaphysics, philosophy, mythology, ethics and ritual.

1. HISTORY OF JAINISM

The Jainas themselves believes that Jainism has exists since eternity and it had like the Jain universe no beginning and would have no end. Most of the saint of Jainism belonged to remote ages; millions and billions year's ago.[1] The word Jaina is derived from *jina* which means conqueror i.e. one who has conquered his passions and desires. Jaina religion may be described, in its very elemental features, as an *Arya* or Indian Sectarian Religion. In the *census* of India, it is stated that " The Jaina religion like Buddhism is held to have been originally an offshoot from Hinduism, and many Jainas still continue to consider themselves as members of the

---

1. Vide, *A History of The Jainas*, P.3.

Hindu community, will intermarry with Hindus and take part in their festivals."[2] Though the origin and growth of the Jainism was the consequence of both pre-*Aryan* and *Aryan* influence but the *Brahmonic* thought and practices also cannot be deny.

Twenty-four *Tirthankaras* are considered as the begineres of the Jaina Philoophical system. The first *Tirthankara* Rsabhadeva is considered as the profounder of this system. The last *Tirthankara* Vardhamana is also known as Mahvira, said to have lived in the 6th century B.C. during the time of Gautama Budha. All the twenty –four Tirthankaras are also known as a *jina.* It is because; they have conquered all passions (raga *and dvesa*) and have attained liberation. Tirthankaras are appeared in the world in different cosmic periods, which consist of an age of evolution and growth, followed by an age of dissolution and decay. The former is called *utsarpini.* The latter is called *avasarpini.* All the twentyfour *Tirthankaras* appeared in the period of *avasarpini.*

A) (a) SIMILARITY AND DIFFERENCES WITH ORTHODOX PHILOSOPHY.

Some similarities have been seen among Jainism and other philosophies. Such as, Like Samkhya and Yoga, Jainism believed in dualism of matter and soul, looks upon worldly life as bad and painful, and holds that liberation from the cycles of birth by the possession of right knowledge is the aim of human life.[4] Jainism rejects the doctrine of the universe and also the theory of creation along with Samkhya, Yoga, Nyaya, Vaisesika and Purva-Mimamsa phylosophy.[5] Jainism considers the world as a product of evolution with the Uttara Mimamsa.[6]

Jainism differs from the Samkhya and the Yoga philosophy in the methods of realizing salvation. [7] Though its believes in dualism of matter and soul, but these metaphysical principles are worked out in different lines in this religion. The

2. Vide, *Census of India*, Vol.I, and P.1.
4. Vide, *Encyclopaedia of Religion and Ethics*, P.465.
5. Vide, *The Cultural Heritage of India*, PP.186-187.
6. Ibid.P.190
7. Vide, *Encyclopaedia of Religion and Ethics*, P.465.

Samkhya has adopted Brahmonical modes of thought, but Jaina has adopted animistic ideas.[8]

(b) SIMILARITY AND DIFFERENCES WITH BUDDHA PHILOSOPHY.

Jainism and Buddhism both are pressismistic and monastic religious.[9] Both considers the world as an abode of sorrow and held that salvation is the aim of human life.[10] Both deny the authenticity of the vedas as an infallible authority and question the efficacy of the rites prescribed in them for the purpose of salvation.[11]

Jainism differs from Buddhism on various ways. Such as, Jainism advocates the possession of right belief, right knowledge and right conduct as a means to the attainment of *nirvana*, [12] but Buddhism suggests the eight fold path as a means to this end.[13] Buddhism denies the existence of soul but Jainism believes the existence of soul.[14]

B) MEANING AND HISTORY OF THE TERM TIRTHANKARA:

Regarding meaning of the term *Tirthankara* different opinions have been given by the Jaina followers. The word *Tirthankara* is derived from the root '*tri*' in the sense of '*tarane*'. The word 'tirtha', derived from this root which meaning is bridge. Thus *Tirthankara* is a bridge maker.[15]Svetambara and Digambara defines that *Tirthankara* is a prophet. A *Tirthankara* is always free-form all the cause of bondage of this ocean of samsara or transmigration can be crossed.Some Jaina followers opines, *pravacana* or sound teaching is the meaning of *tirtha*. As this *pravacana* is found without fail in a *samgha* or church, so a *samgha* is called *Tirtha* and a *Tirthankara* is one who founds the church or *samgha* [16]

8. Ibid, P.465.
9. Vide, *Indias Past*, P.68.
10. Vide, Ancient India, P.168.
10. Ibid.
11. Ibid.
12. Vide, *The Cultural Heritage of India*, P.195.
13. Vide, *Religions of India*, PP 305-306.
14. Vide, *The Cultural Heritage of India*, P.195.
15. Vide, A study in the Origin and Development of Jainism. P.10.
16. taranti yena samsarasagaram iti tirtham pravacanam
     tadvyatire kadeva samghas tirtham tatkaranasilatvattirthankarah .
     Bhagavati Sutra, Vide, *The Jaina Iconography*. P.11.

Another authority believes that the Jaina Tirthankaras were deified heroes, born of human parents who were raised to the position of God by their renunciation and great services to religion for the deliverance of mankind.[17]

Above all some Jaina philosophers describe that *Tirtha* means *Dharma* and one who expounds *Dharma is* called *Tirthankara*. They are the founders of their religion.[18]

Tirthankaras are Gods for the followers of the Jainas. They occupy highest position in Jainism due to their great service deliverance of mankind. They are regarded as guides and spiritually great souls.The liberated souls who go up to the top of the universe and remain there for even in the state of absolute perfection. The Jainas beliefs that each *Tirthankara* is a separate individual –a perfect soul. The Tirthankaras keep their individual identity even after their liberation from physical body, he, like other liberated souls residing in that part of the universe, is called a siddha.[19]

The lives of the Tirthankaras are found in different books. The earliest reference to the twenty four tirthamkaras has been made in the *Samvaya*, the *Kalpasutra*, and the *Avasyaka Niryukti*.[20] A study of Jaina works like Hemchandra's *Trisastisalakapurusacarita* reveals that the life of the twenty four Tirthankaras ran almost on identical lines. All the Tirthankaras were born in Kstriya royal families. All were averse to worldly life. All of them had very long lives, except Mahavira, most of them ruled for a long time. They practiced asceticism and attained moksa after founding a community of disciples. According to the Jaina works the *Samvaya*, the *Kalpasutra*, and the *Avasyaka, Niryukti* , Rsabha, the first *Tirthankara,* was in the third age, i.e. the periods of happiness and sorrow, and the remaining twenty-three

17. loyassujjoyayare sudhammtitthakare jine vand *I* arahante
    kittaise cauvisam ceva kevalino *II Samayikapatha,*
    Vide The *Jaina Iconography,* P. 12.
18. tirtham dharmam karoti prakatayati iti tirthankarah.
    svatirthanamadikartarah tirthakarah.Ibid.
19. Vide, *Aspects of Jaina Art and Architecture.* P. 4.
20. Vide, *The Cultural Heritage of India,* PP.186-187.

Tirthankaras were born in the fourth age, i.e. the period of sorrow and happiness .[21] Of the twenty-four Tirthamkaras, twenty-two have been ascribed to the *Iksavaku* dynasty of the Ksatriyas. [22]But the Munisurvata and Neminathaare said to have belonged to the Yadeva dynasty of the Ksatriyas. Some *carita* and *Purana* books gives the lives of the Tirthankaras. The life of Rsabha is found in *Adipurana* and Uttarapurana describes other Jainas.Bhavadeva Suries Parsvanathacarita, Sakalakirti's Santinathacarita, Vijayagan's Aristanemicarita, Krsnadada's Vimalanathapurana, Brahmanemidatta's Neminathapurana etc, are some other works where the life of the Tirthankara's are found. Yaksa, Sasanadevata, Laksmi, Ganesa, Yaksini etc deities are also worshipped by the Jainas.

b) THE LIVES OF THE TIRTHANKARAS:

1.RSABHADEVA:- The earliest *Tirthankara* of Jainism was Rsabhadeva also known as Adinatha, who was born in the womb of Marudevi. Nabhi was his father . His name Rsabha came due to his mother's dream before his birth, where she had seen that a bull coming towards her.[23] The *Bhagavata Purana* says that not only as the first teacher of Jainas, but also as one of the twenty-four incarnations of Visnu.[24] He preserves two symbols, one is Bull and other is Dharmacakra. The tree connected with his *kevalajnana* is Nyagrodha. The name of his Yaksa and Yaksini are Gomukha and Yaksini cakresvari.

2.AJITA : Ajita was born in *Ayodhya* in the womb of Vijayasenadevi and he is regarded as the second *Tirthankara.* Before his birth his mother saw an elephant in her several dreams. In Indian faith an elephant is connected with kingly power. After his birth all his father's enemies were conquered (*Jita*), hence his name, the invincible one.[25] The symbol related to him is an elephant and his special tree is

21. Vide, *Life in Ancient India as Depicted in Jaina Canons.* P.371.
22 Vide, *Encyclopaedia of Religion and Ethics*, P.466.
23. urvorvrrsabhalanchanmabhud bhagavato jananya ca caturdasanam svapnanamadavrsabho drstastena rsabhah . Ibid, P 36.
24. Vide, *Bhagavata Purana*, 5.4.6.
25. devim vijayasenakhyam sodasasvapnapurvakam *I*
pravisantam vilokyatmavaktrabjam gandhasindhuram *II* UP,
Vide, *The Jaina Iconography.* P.37.

Kevalavrksa. The tree connected with his *Kevala-jnana* is *Kevala-vrksa.* Mahayaksa and Ajitabala are his Yaksa and Yaksni .

3.SAMBHAVANATHA;-The third *Tirthankara, s*ambhavanatha was the son of king Drdharaja and queen Susena , born in Sravasati. His king father had been distressed to see the way his dominions were ravaged by plague and famine, but when he heard the good news of his child birth, he felt that there was a chance of better times coming (*sambhava*). So he has been known as Sambhavanatha.26 His symbol is Horse. The tree under which he received the *Kevala*-knowledge is *Sala.* Trimukha and Duritari were the name of his Yaksa and Yakasini.

4.ABHINANDANA: Abhinandana, the fourth *Tirthankara* of Jainism was the son of Svayamvara and Siddhartha who lived in *Ayodhya.* He was so called because Indra used to come down to the earth to worship him.[27]He preserves the symbol of an ape. Under *piyala* tree he received the *Kevala* knowledge. The name Yaksa and Yaksini related to him were Isvar and Kali respectively.

5.SUMATINATHA: Sunmatinatha, the fifth sage of Jainism comes from a Rajput family. His parents were Megharatha and Mangala. He was born in *Kankanapura.* The child was called Sumatinatha, because before the birth of the child, his mother's intellect (*Sumati*) was so sharpened. A story is related that there was an old Brahmin , having two wives and a son. After his death, both wives claimed that the only son was belonged to each of them and always quarreled had been seen between them. Ultimately the matter was laid before the Queen for settlement. The Queen gave a intelligence ordered that to end of the dispute the living child should be cut into two pieces .[28] So, he was named as Sumatinatha. Heron was his symbol and the tree connected with his *Kevala* knowledge was *Priyamgu* and Tumbaru is his Yaksa and Mahakali was his Yaksini.

---

26. garbhasthe'smin dhyute rajna janani na jitetyajitasam sukham
    bhavatyasmin stute sambhavah /
    yadva garbhagate'pyasminnabhyadhikayasya sambhavat sambhavo'pi /Ibid,39
27. abhinandyate devendradibhirityabhinandanah. Ibid, P.40.
28. sobhana matiryasya sumatih *I*
    yadva garbhasthe jananyah suniscita matirbhuditi sumatih *II* Ibid, P.42.

6. PADMAPRABHA: Kausambi was ruled by a Rajput king whose name was Dhara and his great son Padmaprabha was known as sixth *Tirthankara* of Jainism. His name became Padmaprabha because his mother Susima had a desire to lie down on the bed of lotuses before

the birth of the child.[29] *Kevala* tree related to him was *chatrabha*. The names of his Yaksa and the Yaksini were known as Kusuma and Syama respectively.

7.SUPARSVANATHA: Suparsvanatha, the seventh *Tirthankara* of Jainism was the son of Supratistha and Prthivi . Banaras was known as his birth place. He was endowed from birth with beautiful sides so he was known by the name Suparsava. Moreover, his mother was suffering from leprosy disease. She cured from this before his birth and therefore he was given the name of *su* (good) and *parsva* (sides).[30] The Yaksa and Yaksini related to him were Matanga and Santi respectively. *Sirisa* and *Svastika* were his *kevala* tree and symbol.

8. CANDRAPRABHA: The eight *Tirthankara* of Jainism was Candraprabha whose parents were Rajputs and they belonged to Candrapuri . Before his birth, his mother longed to drink the moon and when he was born, he was found as bright as the moon and his name became Candraprabha.[31] The moon became symbol of him. The tree connected with his *kevala* knowledge was *Naga*. Vijaya and Bhrkuti were the names of his Yaksa and Yaksini.

9.SUVIDHINATHA: The nineth *Tirthankara* was Suvidhinatha, son of Sugriva and Rama. His place of *Nirvana* was *Sameta-sikhara*. Before his birth his kingly relatives were warring against one another, but after his birth they gave up fighting between themselves and took to performing religious duties . His birth eventually brought *Suvidhi* . (good order) [32] to the distracted family and so his name became Suvidhinatha. He was also called Puspadanta due to his beautiful teeth which was like the buds of flowers. Two different opinions had been seen about his symbol

---

29. Vide, *Heart of Jainism*, P.52
30. sobhanau parsvavasya suparsvah. Vide, *The Jaina Iconography*, P.44
31. Vide, *Heart of Jainism*, 53.
   cf. tatha garbhasthe devyah candrapanadohado'bhuditi
   candraprabhah. Vide, The *Jaina Iconography*, P.45.
32. sobhano vidhirvidhanamasya suvidhih.Ibid.P.46.

and *kevala* tree. The Svetambara belived that dolphin was his symbol but the Digambaras believed that crab was his symbol. Regarding the tree under which he attained the *kevala* knowledge was the *Naga,* according to some authorities and another authority, it was *Malli.* Ajita and Sutari Devi were Yaksa and Yaksini of this sage.

      10. SITALANATHA: King Drdharatha and Queen Sunanda's son Sitalanatha became the tenth *Tirthankara* of Jainism. He acquired a marvellous power to cure fever and bring coolness to the patients. His father was suffering from fever where all the physicians had given up all hopes of his recovery. But when he was in his mother
Womb, his mother laid her hand on her husband and immediately fever left him and father was cured and then he came to know as Sitalanatha.[33]His symbol and *Kevala* tree was *Srivatsa-svastika* and *Vilva.* Brahma and Asoka are the his Yaksa and Yaksini.

      11.SREYAMSANATHA: Sreyamsanatha, the eleventh *Trithankara* was the son of king Visnudeva and Visnudri. It had been found that his father had a very beautiful and peculiar throne .But unfortunately an evil spirit took up his abode in it, so that no one even dared to sit on it. Then his mother before the birth of child, however, made up her mind to sit on it. When she sat on it, nothing untoward happened. So his name was made Sreyamsanatha the lord of good.[34] Rhinoceros was his symbol and *Tumbara was the* tree connected with his *kevela jnana.* Yakseta and Manavi are his Yaksa and Yaksini .

      12.VASUPUJYA: The twelfth *Tirthanikara* who born in Campapuri was Vasupujya and he was the son of Vasupujya and Jayavati .His name has been derived in two ways. First, due to son of Vasupujya, he was called Vasupujya. And secondly, before his birth the Gods Indra and Vasu came to worship his father and

33. tatha garbhasthe bhagavati pituh purvotpanna
    cikitsyapittadaho jananikarasparsadupasanta iti sitalah. Ibid, P.47.
34. yatha garbhasthe'smin kenapyanakrantapurva devata' dhisthitasayya   jananya kranteti sreyo
    jatamiti   sreyamsah. Ibid.,P.48.

brought for him wealth (*vasu*) from heaven. [35] Male buffalo was his symbol .
Regarding *kevala* tree one believes *Patalika* and another believes *Kadamba*.
Kumara and Canda were the Yaksa and Yaksini .

13.VIMALANATHA:- The thirteenth *Tirthankara*, Vimalanatha was the
son of the king Krtavarman and Suramya . He is known as Vimalanath (Lord of
clearness) after the clearness of intellect of his mother with which she was endowed
before his birth.[36] Boar was his sign and *Jambu* was his *kevala* tree . Sanmukha and
Vairoti was Yaksa and Yaksini.

14.ANANTANATHA: Anantanatha became fourteenth *Tirthankara* of
Jainism who was the son of Simhasena and Jayasyama. His mother saw an endless
(*ananta*) necklace of pearls in a dream before his birth and so he was named as
Anantanatha.[37]The svetambaras believed hawk was his symbol and the Digambaras
believed bear was his symbol. Asvattha was his *kevela*. Patata and Anantamati were
the Yaksa and yaksini.

15. DHARMANATHA: Bhanuraja and Suvrata's son
Dharmanatha became the fifteenth *Tirthankara* of Jainism. Before his birth his
mother performed many religious rites while he was in her womb. And therefore
after his born he was known as Dharmanatha.[38]Thunder bolt was his symbol .The
kevela-tree was called *Dadhiparana* or sapta- cchada. Kinnara and Kandarpa are his
Yaksa and Yaksini.

16. SANTINATHA: The sixteenth *Tirthankara* Santinatha was the son of
Visvasena and Acira born at *Hastinapura*. He was named as Santinatha or Lord of
peace due to his birth peace brought to the place.[39] Deer was his symbol . Under
Nandi Vrksa tree he received the *kevala* knowledge. Kimpurusa and Mahamanasi
were the Yaksa and Yaksini of him.

35. vasupujyanrpaterayam vasupujyah *I* yadva garbhasthe'smin
vasu hiranyam tena vasavo rajakulam pujitavaniti. vasavo
devavisesah tesam pujyo va vasupujyah, prajnadyani
vasupujyah. Ibid, P.49.
36. vigato malo'sya vimalajnananadiyogadva vimalah. yadva-
garbhasthe maturmatistanusca vimala jateti vimalah. Ibid.,P.50.
37. Vide, *Heart of Jainism* P.55.
38. Ibid.
39. tatha garbhastha purvotpannasivasantirbhuditi santih. Vide, *TheJaina Icongraphy* , P 52

9

17. KUNTHUNATHA:- The seventeenth *Tirthankara* was Kunthunatha ,the son of king Sivaraja and Sridevi. He was known by the name due to his mothers dream before his birth, where she had seen a large heap (*kuntha*) of jewels.[40] His symbol was a goat. The tree under which he attained the kevala- knowledge was *Tilakataru*. The Yaksa and the Yaksini related to him were Gandharva and Bala.

18.ARANATHA:-The eighteenth sage Arnatha was the son of king Sudarsana and Mitrasena Devi. His mother saw a wheel (*Ara*) of Jewels in her dream so he obtained the name of Aranatha.[41] *Svastika* was his symbol. The sacred tree related to him was mango tree. The Yaksa and the Yaksini were Yaksendra and Dharani Devi.

19.MALLI:- The nineteenth *Tirthankara* was Malli. Svetambaras believed that Mali was a woman and was the daughter of king Kumbha and Prajavati. She was known as Malli because before her birth her mother had desired to wear a garland of flowers called *Mallika*.[42] Her symbol was a water –jar. The tree under which she attained *kevala*- knowledge was *Asoka*. Kubera and Dharanapriya were the Yaksa and Yaksini of her. Digambaras , denies this belief of the Svetambaras. Their faith is that no woman can ever be liberated and subsequently become a *Tirthankara*. Therefore they believed that nineteenth *Tirthankara* was also a male.

20. MUNISUVRATA:- Munisuvrarta was the son of King Sumitra and Sama. Before his birth his mother Sama observed all the vows of Jainism. After birth of the child, he was given the name of Munisuvrarta .[43] Tortoise was his symbol. He obtained *kevalajnana* under *Campaka* tree. Varuna and Naradatta were the Yaksa and the Yaksini of him.

---

40. tatha garbhasthe bhagavati janani ratnanam kunthurasim
drstavatiti kunthuh, Ibid, P.53.
41.tatha garbhasthe bhagavati jananya svapne sarvaratnamayo'ro drsta ityarah Ibid,P 54

42.tatha garbhasthe bagavati matuh surabhikusumamalyasayaniyadohado
devalaya purita mallih .Ibid,P.55.
43. sobhanani vratanyasya suvratah muniscasau suvratasca munisuvratah, Ibid. P.56

21.NAMINATHA:-Naminatha, the twentyfirst *Tirthankara* was the son of Vijayaraja and Vappila. The enemies of his father bowed down in submission when he was in his mother's womb and therefore he was named as Naminatha. [44]Blue lotus was his symbol and Bakula was *kevala* tree. Bhrukti and Gandhari were his Yaksa and Yaksini respectively.

22.NEMINATHA or ARISTANEMI:- Neminath or Aristanemi was the twentysecond *Tirthankara* of the Jainas who was the son of Samudra-Vijaya and Sivadevi. Before his birth his mother saw a wheel *(nemi)* of black jewels(*arista*) so his name became Aristanemi.[45] Conchshell was his symbol. The tree related to his *kevalajnana* is Mahavenu. The *Yaksa* and *Yaksini* are Gomedha and Ambika.

23.PARSAVANTHA:- The twenty fourth Tirthankara Parsavanatha was the son of Asvasena and Vama. He was known by the name because when he was in the womb of his mother, she saw a serpent crawling by her side.[46]At the age of 30, Parsavanatha renounced the world and became an ascetic. He practiced penance for eighty-three days . On the eighty-fourth day, he obtained *Kevala-jnana*. He preached the truth for about 70 years and achieved salvation or Moksa at the age of 100 years on the Mount Parsvanatha in Bengal. Snake is his symbol. The *Devadaru* was his *kevala*-tree. Parsva or Vamana and Padmavati was his Yaksa and Yaksini.

24. MAHAVIRA : The last *Tirthankara* was Known as Mavahara, also known as Vardhamana, who was the greatest of all *Tirthankara* of Jainism . Mahavira was the second son of Siddhartha a *ksatriya* chieftain of *Magadha* and Trisala . He was born in the village called *Kundagrama* near Vaisali about 599 B.C.He was called *Kundagrama* near Vaisali about 599 B.C. He was called Vardhamana because before his birth, his family's treasures were increasing day byday.[47] He sustained all fears and dangerous and endured all hardships and calamities. So he was called Mahavira by the Gods.[48]

---

44. yadva garbhasthe bhagavati paracakranrapairapi pranatih krteti namih. Ibid., P.57.
45. Vide, *Heart of Jainism* PP.57-58.
46. tatha garbhasthe jananya nisi sarpo drsta iti garbhanubhavo'yamiti matva pasyatit niruktatparsvah .Vide, *The Jaina Iconography.P.60.*
47. Vide, *Jaina philosophy* , P.8
48. *Ibid.*

Mahavira was lived as a householder for thirty years. But, when his parents died, he left his home and became an ascetic at the age of 30. After twelve years of constant meditation, he went to a place known as *Trmbhikagrama* which was near Parsvanatha hills. In that place sitting under the shade of a *Sala* tree by the side of the river *Rjuvallika,* he mediated deeply for some time and ultimately attained the absolute or perfect knowledge *(kevala-jnana)* .After this he was regarded omniscient and a *Tirthankara*[49] He died in 527 B.C., at the age of 72. Lion was his symbol and *Sala* was *kevala* tree. The Yaksa and Yaksini were named as Matanga and Siddhayika .

2 . TWO SECTS OF JAINISM

The Svetambara and the Digamgbara are the two sects of the *Jain* community. They are again sub-divided into three number of sub- sects. The sub-division Svetambara are (I) Murtipujaka, (II) Sthanakavasi, and (III) Terapanthi. And (I) Bisapanthi, (II) Terapanthi and (III) Taranapanthi are the sub-divisons of Digamgbara.

There are no fundamental differences of doctrines between the two divisions. Both the sects have same religious and philosophical beliefs and practically the same mythology but some minor differences have been seen even amongst these sub-divisions.

The differences were only on some minor details of Jaina religious faith and practice. The teaching of the *Jinas* are accepted by the both the sects. The monks belonged to the Svetambara group wear white clothes and Digambara group wear no clothes. The literal meaning of the word Svetambara is white –clad, whereas Digambara is sky-clad.

The following are the main points of differences among them are :

1. Two sects have different opinion regarding the food of the *kevali* (omniscient). The *Digambaras* maintain that a *kevali* does not need any intake of food, while the *Svetambaras* think that they do. The point is academic, for both the sects are unanimous that nobody is going to become a *Kevali* in the foreseeable future.

2. Another difference between the two sects is that the *Digambaras* think that all *Jain* ascetics should follow the example of Mahavira and remain nude, while the Svetambaras think that the practice of remaining nude known as *JinaKalpa* was given up by the great teachers of the church within a few generations after Mahavira (i.e. after Jambu) and they had started wearing white garments. This practice was known as *sthaviraKalpa*. The present-day ascetics according to the *Svetambaras* need follow only these great teachers (*sthaviras*), and it was necessary to practice the *JinaKalpa.*

3. The Digambaras group believes that women cannot obtain liberation but the Svetambaraas does not believe it.

4. The Svetambaras believed that Puspapadanta, who was the ninth *Tirthankara*, had a dolphin as a symbol but the Digambaras think that it was the crab.

5. The Svetambaras believed Malli ,the nineteenth *Tirthankara,* was a woman. The Digambaras believed that as it was not possible for a woman to become a *Tirthankara* ,so Malli was a male.

3. RELIGIOUS AND PHILOSOPHICAL LITERATURE, OF THE JAINAS :

Jainism literature has been found in two different languages, mostly in Prakrt and ae well as in Sanskrit. Most of the early literature is not available now.There is a difference between the Svetambaras and Digambaras regarding their canonical literature . The Svetambaras hold that there were originally two kind of sacred books, Viz, (I) the fourteen Purvas and (II) the twelve *Angas*. Besides the 12 *angas,* there are 12 *Upangas,* 10 *Prakinas,* 6 *Chedasutras, Nandi* and *Anuyogaddvara ,* and 4 Mulasutras.

1. The fourteen Purvas are (i) *Utpada,* (ii) *Agraniya,*(iii) *Viryapravada,* (iv*) Astinastipravada,* (v) *Jnanapravada,* (vi) *Satyapravada,* (vii) *Atma –pravada,* (viii) *Karmapravada,* (ix) *Pratyakhyana,* (x) *Vidyanuvada,* (xi) *Kalyana,* (xii) *Pranavaya,* (xiii) *Kriyavisala,* and (xiv) *Trilokabindusara.*

13

2.The twelve *Angas* are: (i) *Acara* , (ii) *Sutrakrata*, (iii) *Sthana*, (iv) *Samavaya*, (v) *Bhagavati*, (vi) *Jnata-dharmakatha*, (vii) *Upasakadas*, (viii) *Antakrddasa* (ix) *Anuttaraupapatiksadas*, *(x)* *Prasnavyakarana*, (xi) *Vipaka* and (XII) *Drstivada* .

3.The twelve *Upangas* are(i) *Aupapatika*, (ii) *Rajaprasniya*, (iii) *Jivabhigama*, (iv)*Prajnapana*, (v) *Jambudvipaprajnapti* (vi) *Candraprajnapti*, (vii) *Suryaprajnapti*, (viii) *Niryavalika*, (ix) *kalpavatamsika*,(x) *Puspikah*, (xi) *Puspaculikah*, and (xii*)Vrsnidasah*.

4.The ten Prakinas as are : (i) *Catuhsarana*, (ii) *Samstara*, (iii) *Aturapratyakhyana*, (iv) *Bhaktaparijna*, (v)*Tandulavaiyali*, (vi) *Candavija*,(vii)*Devndrastava*,(viii)*Ganivija*,(ix) *Mahapratyakhyana*, (x) *Virastava*,

5. The six Chedasutras are: (i) *Nisitha*, (ii) *Mahanisitha*, (iii) *Vyavahara*,(iv)*Dasasrutaskandha*,(v)*Brhatkalpa*,and (vi) *Pancakalpa*.

6. There two sutras are (I) *Nandi* and (II) *Anuyogadvara* .

7. The four Mulasutras are : (i) *Uttaradhyana*, (ii) *Avasyaka*, (iii) *Dasavaikalika*, and (iv) *Pindaniryukti*.

It is not easy to give an account of the canonical works of the Digambaras. The Digambaras canonical literature is divided into two groups, viz, (I) *Angapravista* and (II) *Angabahya*. The *Angapravista* is of twelve kinds which are similar to the twelve Angas of the Svetambaras. They   also recognize the fourteen Purvas. The *Angabahya* text are those which do not belong to the Angas. The *Angabahya* is of fourten kinds .Such texts are : (I) *Samayika, (II) Vandana*, (III) Samstava,(IV) *Pratikramana (V) Vinaya,(VI) Krtikarama,(VII) Dasavaikalika, (VIII) Uttaradhyayana (IX) kalpavyavahara, (X) Kalpakalpa, (XI) Mahakalpa sanjnaka, (XII) Pundarika, (XII) Mahapundarika and (XIV) Nisiddhika.*

As the works belonging to the canon are of different origin and age, they differ greatly in character. Some are chiefly in prose, some in verse, an some in both prose and verse. A large number of commentaries have grown up round the sacred texts. And besides these, the Jainas also possess a seculiar literature of their own in poetry and prose, both in Sanskrit and Prakrit. The oldest Prakrt poem , the *Paumacariya,* is a Jaina version of the *Ramayana.* There are also many Jaina moral tales and dramas. The Jaina authors have also contributed many works, original treatises as well as commentaries, to the scientific literature of India in its various branches Viz. grammar, biography, poetics, philosophy etc. It may here be mentioned that the Jainism also possesses a many works on Jaina Nyaya philosophy. There are many writers who wrote their works on Jaina Nyaya philosophy. Kundakunda, the great *acharya* and prolific writer of books on Jainism was living in the first century AD. Kundakunda wrote in *Prakrit* (which was akin to *Shauraseni6* i.e., the language of the Mathura region) and this would be a language quite unfamiliar to the local people other than the learned among the *Jain*s. Kundakunda is one of the famous Jaina philosopher. The *Pavayanasara Pancastikayasara, Samayasara* and *Niyamasara* etc. are his valuable works.

The most celebrated *acharya* among the *Digambaras* after Kundakunda was Umasvami. Umasvami or Umasvali is said to have been a prolific writer and said to have written about 500 books. Very few of these are known today. The Digambars think that the 14 *Pujaprakarna Prasamarati*, and *Jambudvipasamasa* are his work. His greatest work the *Tattvarthadhigamasutra* is a manual work for understanding the true nature of the things. It deals with the Jaina logic, episteomology, ethics etc. There are many commentaries on *Tattvarthadhigamasutra.* The following among them are worthy of special mention ;

1. *Sarvarthasiddhi* of Pujyapada Devanandi in 5th century.

2. *Tattvartharajavarttika* of Akalanka in 7th century.

3. *Tattvarthaslokvarttika* of Vidyananda in 9th century.

Siddhasena Divakara is also one of the noted Jaina philosopher. His valuable works are : *Sanmatitarka, Nyayavatara* etc. The *Nyayavatara* is the earliest Jaina work on pure logic. He has made a valuable contribution to Jaina philosophical literature.

Another author Samantabhadra, was a *Digambara* and he wrote a commentary of Umasvami's Tattvartha Dhigama*Sutra*. The main part of the commentary is no longer extant but the introductory part of the commentary exists. It is known as Devagama-*Sutra* or Aptamimansa. On this work, Akalankadeva wrote a commentary entitled *Astasati*. Vidyananda also wrote a commentary on *Astasati* entitled *Astasahasri*. Yuktyanusasana is another important work of *Samantabhadra*.

Akalankadeva, the great Jaina writer developed the subject of Jaina Nyaya philosophy elaborately in his work like *Tattvartharajavarttika, Astasati, Loghiyastraya, Pramanasangraha* etc.

Prariksamukhasutram is one of the famous work on Jaina Nyaya. Manikyanandi is the author of this famous book. It is written in aphorisms style. One of the famous commentary on *Prariksamukhasutram* is *Prameyakamalamartanda* of Prabhacandra.

4. LIFE AND TIME OF PRABHACANDRA:

Prabhacandra was a Jaina philospher belonged to 11th century. He is also a grammarian. But nothing detail is known about his life and time. From his book *Prameyakamalamartanda* , it is known only about the name of his guru and the place where he written his work. Padmanandi Saiddhanta was his *guru*.[50] From his logical work, it can also be known that Prabhacandra written this book on *Dharanagari* where ruled Bhojadeva. [51]Though his time had not been mentioned in his book, yet it can be derived his time after 8th century and before 9th century from different kind of sources. Janasena, the author of *Adipurana* stated the name and time of a Prabhacandra, who wrote *Candrudaya*.[52]From the name of *Candrudaya* , everyone accepts it is a *Nyayakumudacandra* of Prabhacandra .But, the original name of the work is *Nyayakumudacandra* not *Candrudaya*. so, the author of *Nyayakumudacandra* and *Candrudaya* are not same. Jinasena who completed the

50. sripadmanandisaiddhanasisyo'nekagunalayah /
    prabhacandras'chiram jiyadratnanandipade ratah// PKM.P.694.
51. sribhojadevarajye -----vivrtamiyi. Ibid.
52. Ibid., P.58

16

commentary of *Jayadhavala* of his guru virasena in 759 A.D. after that he completed *Adipurana* in 840 A.D. For that reason,every scholar accepted the time of Prabhacandra after 8th century and before 9th century. [53] But there are some doubts about this time, Firstly some arguments are put below for this reason:

1. One of the most famous *Purana* i.e. Harivamsapurana was written by Jinasena in 783 A.D. It was earlier than the *Adipurana*. In that *Purana* he mentioned the name of Prabhacandra who was a pupil of Kumarsena and also described him as a *Candrudaya* like the *Adipurana*.[54] From that point of view, it can be said that these two person i.e. Prabhacandra are the same person and a pupil of Kumarsena. So, Prabhacandra, the greatest philosophical author of *Prameyakamalamartanda* and *Nyayakumudacandra* is different from that Prabhacandra, which found in the two puranas i.e. the *Adipurana* and the *Harivamsapurana*. It is because his guru is Padmanandi Saiddhanta.

2. The writers who followed Akalanka such as Vidyananda and Anantavirya are mentioned by Prabhacandra in his work. But the author of *Adipurana* i.e. Jinasena does no mention the name of Vidyananda and Anantavirya in his work. These two writers also does not belong earlier to 9th century.[55] If prabhacandra belongs earlier to 9th century, then it is not possible for him to mention the name of Vidyananda and Anantavirya in his work. So, prabhacandra does not belong earlier to 9th century.

From the above arguments, it can be said that the author of *Candrudaya* i.e. Prabhacandra is different from that Prabhacandra of *Prameyakamalamartanda*, and the time of Prabhacandra that is mentioned in the *Adipurana* is not a real time.

Now, the time of prabhacandra's is discussed again by mentioning some other works in his *Prameyakamalamartanda* and *Nyayakumudacandra*. Some arguments are put forward for the experiment of his time.

53. Ibid.
54. Vide, *Nyayakumudacandra*, P.118.
55. Ibid.

1. Sakatayana, the followers of Jainism is the author of *Sakatayanavyakarana, Kevalibhukti* and *Strimuktiprakarana*. He wrote commentary on *Sakatayanavyakarana* by the name of *Amoghvrtti*. This commentary was written in the time of ruling king Amoghavarsa. The time of ruling king Amoghavarsa was between 814 A.D. to 877 A.D. Prabhacandra mentioned *Strimuktiprakarana* of Sakatayana in his famous logical work i.e. *Prameyakamalamartanda* and *Nyayakumudacandra*.[56] From that point, it can be said that Prabhacandra does not belong earlier to 9th century. He belongs later to 9th century.

2. Devasena is one of the great historical author or follower of Jainism. He was the writter of famous work like *Darsanasara*. He completed this work in 933 A.D. After that he wrote another work *Bhavasangraha* in 940 A.D.[57]

In *Prameyakamalamartanda* , Prabhacandra mentioned a sloka from *Bhavasangraha* in connection to explain the *Kevalaharavicara*[58] So, Prabhachandra belongs later to 9th century.

3. Abhayanandi, one of the famous author of Jainism was written Jainendramahavrtti in 960 A.D. [59] *Sabdambhojabhaskara* (a work on jainendravyakarana) was written by Prabhacandra . On this ground, Prabhacandra belongs later to 960 A.D.

4. Sridhara is one of the famous author of Vaisesika philosophy. He wrote commentary on *Prasastapadabhasya* called *Nyayakandli* in 991 A.D. [60] In *Prameyakamalamartanda*, Prabhacandra mentioned the Vaisesika work *Nyayakandali* in respect to explain the nature of liberation.[61]So, Prabhacandra belongs later to 9th century.

5. Vadiraja, the famous author or follower of Jainism was the writer of Parsvacarita. Vadiraja completed this work in 1025 A.D.[62] He composed a commentary *Nyayaviniscayavivarana* on *Nyayaviniscayaprakarana* of Akalanka.

56. Vide *Prameyakamalamartanda, P.62*
57. Ibid., P.63
58. Ibid., P.300.
59. Ibid., P.63.
60. Ibid., P.14.
61. Ibid., P.318.
62. Ibid., P.65

Vadiraja does not mention Prabhacandra and his work *Prameyakamalamartanda* in his Parsvacarita. So, Prabhacandra belongs later to 1025 A.D.

6. Syadvadaratnakara, the famous work of Jainism was written by Vadidevasuri in 1118 A.D. He belonged to 12 th century. He mentioned the famous logical work *Prameyakamalamartanda* in his work.[63] From that reason, Prabhacandra belongs earlier than Vadidevasuri. Prabhacandra belonged to 11th century.

7. The most important works on Nyaya and Vaisesika philosophy are *Nyayamanjari* of Jayantabhatta, Vyomvatitika of Vyomsiva and *Loksanavali* of Udayana. The nature of liberation and its refutation that is found in the *Vyomvatitika* of Vyomsiva also found in the *Prameyakamalamartanda* of prabhacandra.[64].
Vyomsiva belonged to 7th century. So, Prabhacandra belongs later. Udayana mentioned the name of Vyomsiva in his work Laksanavali, which was completed in 984 A.D. [65]So, Prabhacandra belongs later.

8. One of the most famous work on nyaya philosophy is *Nyayamanjari* of Jayantabhatta. In *Nyayamanjari,* Jayantabhatta explain one kind of *pramana* known as *Karakasakalyavada*. This *Karakasakalyavada* is refuted by Prabhacandra in his famous logical work i.e *Prameyakamalamartanda* .[66]

Jayantabhatta mentioned the name of Vacaspatimisra, the author of Tatparyatika and *Nyayasucinibandha* in his work. Vacaspatimisra completed in *Nyayasucinibandha* in his work in 841 A.D. For that reason, Jayantabhatta belongs to 9th century. So, Prabhacandra belongs later to 9th century.

9. The another author of Nyaya philosophy is Abhinavadharmabhusana. He was written Nyayadipika in 1384 A.D. [67] He belonged to 14th century. He mentioned the greatest logical work *Prameyakamalamartanda* and his author Prabhacandra in his work. From that point of view, Prabhacandra belongs erlier than Abhinavadharmabhusana.

63. Ibid., P.66.
64. Ibid., P.307.
65. Ibid., P.13.
66. Ibid., P.7.
67. Ibid., P.65.

10. Mallisena is one of the Jaina philosophers. He was the author of *Syadvadamanjari*, which completed in 1293 A.D. He belonged to 13 century. In *Syadvadamanjari*, he mentioned Prabhacandra and his work Nyayakumudacandra.[68] So, Prabhacandra belongs earlier than Mallisena.

11.Hemacandra is the most versatitle Jaina writer. He belonged to 12 century. The *Pramanamimamsa* is a valuable work on Jaina logic by Hemacandra. Hemacandra mentioned the greatest logical work *Prameyakamalamartanda* and his author Prabhacandra in his work.[69] From that point of view Prabhacandra belongs earlier than Hemacandra.

From the above point of discussion,it may be said that Prabhacandra does not belongs earlier to 9th or 10th century.He belonged to 11th century.

a) WORKS OF PRABHACANDRA

Prabhacandra is the author of very voluminous works of Jainism literature. His *Prameyakamalamartanda* is one of the most important work on Jaina philosophy. Another important works of Prabhacandra is Nyayakumudachandra which is a commentary on *Loghistraya* of Akalanka. There are also some other works of prabhacandra such as *Tattvarthavrttipadavivarana* (a commentary of *Sarvarthasiddhi* of Pujyapada), *Sakatayananyasa* (a commentary on *Sakatayanavyakarana)*, *Sabdambhojabhaskara* (a work on *Jainendravyakarana*), *Pravacanasarasarojabhaskara* (a commentary of *Pravacanasara* of Kundakunda) and *Gadyakathakosa*. These commentories are very voluminous and deal with the Jaina system in details.

5. A BRIEF DESCRIPTION OF *PRAMEYAKAMALAMARTANDA*

Prameyakamalamartanda is a comprehensive Sanskrit commentary on *Pariksamukhasutram* (a work on Jaina logic by Manikyanandi). It is known as *Prameyakamalamartanda* because as the lotus will bloom by the sun, in the same way, all the objects of knowledge will express by this work. In *Prameyakamalamartanda*, all the important topics of Jaina philosophy, i.e., the

---

68. Ibid., P.300.
69. Ibid., P.50.

20

reality of knowledge, *viparitakhyativada*, the doctrine of self, *Karma*, liberation, *anekantavada, syadvada, nayavada* etc are discussed.

Prameyakamalamartanda is an encyclopedic work on Indian Philosophy. It is a specific work on Indian logic. It has involved the Nyaya system, the Vaisesika system, the Mimamsa system, the Samkhya system, the Yoga system, the Advaita system, the Buddhist system, the Carvaka system. *Prameyakamalamartanda*, Prabhacandra has not only discussed the Jaina philosophical tenets, but also has refuted all the rival views in order to establish the Jaina view. Prabhacandra systematically presents the *purvapaksa* views and gives thorough and authentic exposition of their views, after that he finally establish the *uttarapaksa* views i.e. the jaina view.

*Prameyakamalamartanda*is divided into six chapters. In the first chapter, the general definition of *Pramana*, the *Karakaskalyavada* of Jayantabhatta's, the *sannikarsa* of Vaisesika's, *Indriyavrttivada* of Samkhya-Yoga, *jnatrvyapara* of Prabhakara, *nirvikalpakapratyaksavada* of Buddhist, *sabdadvaitavada* of Bhartrhari, *akhyativada* of Carvaka, *asatkhyativada* of Buddhist, *prasiddharthakhyativada* of Samkhya, *atmakhyativada* of Yogacara, *anirvacaniyakhyativada* of Jaina, *smrtipramosavada* of Prabhakara, *sunyavada, sakarajnanavada* of Buddhist, *bhutacaitanyavada* of Carvaka, *paroksajnanavada* of Mimamsa etc are discussed.

In the second chapter, *pramanavadas*, nature of *sakti, abhavavicara sarvajnatvavada*, sankhyas *prakritikartritwavada* nature and role of God, nature of liberation, *anekantavada* etc. are discussed.

The third chapter deals agama, mimansakas *sabdvanityatvavaba*, buddhists *apohavada , sphopavada*

In the fourth chapter, all the categories or *padartha* are discussed. In it , the size of the Jaina self is discussed.

The fifth chapter deals with the hetvabhasas. In this chapter, the meaning of hetvabhasa, the division of *hetvabhasas* etc. are discussed.

Finally, the last chapter deals with the Jaina doctrine of *naya* and *saptabhanginaya* . In this chapter, the nature of *naya*, the categories of naya, the nature of *syadvada*, the divisions of *syadvada* etc. are discussed.

In this way, after throughly discussing the philosophical point of views other systems, Prabhacandra establishes the Jaina view in his *Prameyakamalamartanda* throws light upon all the salient features of Jainism. From the point of view of Jaina logic also, it is an important work.

The chapters have been discussed in details in next.

CHAPTER – II
JAINA METAPHYSICS

The term Metaphysics came to usage in the first century B.C. to denote a part of the philosophical heritage of Aristotle. He called this the most important part of his philosophical doctrines. It is the First Philosophy which studies the highest principles of all that exists , which are inaccessible to the senses, comprehensible only to speculative reason, and indespensible for all.[1] In the Philosophy of the Middle ages ,Metaphysics was used to substantiate theology philosophically. In the 16th century ,the term metaphysics was used in the same sense as the term "ontology." According to Descartes, Leibniz, Spinoza and other Philosophers of the 17th century ,Metaphysics was still closely connected with the natural and humanitarian sciences.

Metaphysics forms an important portion of Jaina sacred literature also. It is the theory of reality. The Jaina metaphysic is realistic and pluralistic. It is also relativistic. The Jainas maintain that a thing has got an infinite number of qualities and modes , which is comprehended by valid knowledge .[2] The Jainas hold that every object possesses innumerable positive and negative characters. Every real object embodies in itself an affirmative and a negative aspect synthesized and held together by its own complex nature.

According to the Tattvartha dhigama Sutra , reality (*sat*) is that which consists of three factors: permanence , origination , and decay.[3] This means that there is disappearance in the midst of permanence. A thing maintains its identity and permanence through a continued process of change consisting of origin and decay . Identity and permanence are the midst of variety and change.

1.THE DOCTRINE OF RELATIVE PLURALISM OR ANEKANTAVADA :

Anekantavada is the basic metaphysical view of Jainism. *Anekantavada* is the

1.I . Frolov I . *Dictionary of Philosophy*, P .267.
2.ananatdharmatmakam vastu . anantadharmatmakam eva tattvam .SDSm , as quoted in *Outlines of Indian Philosophy* , P.126.
3. utpadavyayadhrauvyasamyuktam sat . TAS ,5 . 29 .

view of reality as being pluralistic , many-sided,or expressing itself in multiple forms . "It has its root in intellectual tolerance which on its part is founded on the doctrine of *ahimsa* or non violence. This doctrine of *Anekantavada* holds that reality is many sided and that it can be looked at from different standpoints. All the theories of reality propounded by other philosophers are one sided , since they accept some particular aspect of a thing and reject the others . On the other hand *Anekantavada* takes all the different aspects of reality into account and presents a synthetic view of reality, which comprehends all the absolutistic or one sided theories."[4] This theory states that reality is many sided i.e. endowed with diverse or even contradictory characteristics. The Jainas regard all things as *anekanta(na-ekanta)*. This means that nothing can be affirmed or negated absolutely , as all affirmation or negation are true only under certain conditions and limitations.

The Jainas apply this theory of *anekanta* in determining the nature of categories like matter, space, self or *jiva* etc. Matter and *Jiva* are regarded as separate and independent realities. There are innumerable material atoms and innumerable individual selves which are all separately and independently real. And each atom and each self possesses innumerable aspects of its own. Therefore , it is not possible for all, to know all the qualities of a thing. We can know only some qualities of some thing.[5] To know all the aspects of a thing is to become omniscient. Therefore the Jainas say that he who knows all the qualities of one thing, become the knower of all the qualities of all things.[6] Human knowledge is necessarily relative and limited. Our judgments are also relative. Hence , the Jainas put forward this doctrine of *Anekantavada* in order to describe the nature of a things.

Anekantavada is of two types-(i).*Krama* or successive and (ii).*akrama* or simultaneous. According to the *Krama anekantavada ,* a thing is endowed with different characteristics at different points of time, For example, the self is not liberated at one stage and at another point of time it becomes liberated. According to

4. Sinha , K .P . *The Philosophy of Jainism* , P. 9
5. Cf. A Critical Survey of Indian Philosophy , PP.50-51.
6. eko bhavah sarvatha yena drstah sarve bhava sarvatha tena drstah . S M , P . 4

24

the *akrama anekantavada*, a thing possesses different characteristics at the same point of time .For example, the self is eternal in its essence and is ever-changing in its qualities.[7]

Thus *Anekantavada* propounds that a thing is many sided and complex and no one sided view of the thing is absolute. The one-sided viewpoint of a thing is termed by the Jainas as *Nayavada*.

2.THE DOCTRINE OF NAYA:

According to the Jainas , Knowledge is of two forms, viz. *pramana* or knowledge of a thing as it is in itself , and *naya* or Knowledge of a thing in its relation . The doctrine of *nayas* or standpoints is a peculiar feature of the Jaina logic. The *Anekantavada* of the Jainas propounds that things are endowed with innumerable aspects. Accordingly, the things may be apprehended differently from different points of view . And the apprehension of reality from some such particular stand point is called naya.[8] Prabhacandra defines *naya* as "the apprehension which the knower acquires about a part of the object, without discarding the opposite views.[9] A *naya* becomes *nayabhasa* when it discards the opposite views.[10]

The Jainas divide the philosophical stand points into two broad heads-(i).The *Niscayanaya* and (ii).The *Vyavaharikanaya.* Again *naya* is of two kinds (i).*Dravyarthika* and (ii). *Paryayarthika.* The *Dravyarthika* is further divided into three kinds: (i).*Naigama,* (ii).*Samgrah* and (iii).*Vyavahara.* Again , *Paryayarthika* is divided into four kinds (i)*Rjusutra,* (ii) *Sabda,* (iii). *Samabhirudha* and (iv) *Evambhuta.* Thus, in all, there are seven kinds of *nayas* in Jainism.A brief explanation of these *nayas* is given below:

1.*Naigamanaya* : Every object in this world possesses two kinds of properties, viz, *samanya* (general) and *visesa*(separate). That stand point which takes into consideration both these two aspects , viz, the general and specific is called

7.anekanto hi dvedha kramanekantah , akramanekantasca . tatra
kramanekantapeksaya ya eva pragmuktah sa evedanim muktah
samsari cetyavirodhah PKM , ch 2 , P . 326 .
8. ekadesavisistortho nayasya visayo matah , SM quoted in SDS , ch.3.
9. anirakrtapratipakso vastvamsagrahi jnaturabhiprayo nayah . PKM , P . 636.
10. nirakrtapratipaksastu nayabhasah . Ibid .

Naigama. According to this stand point there can be no general quality without the specific, nor can there be any specific characteristic without the general one.[11]

2.*Samgrahanaya* : The second *naya* is *Samgrahanaya.* That stand point which looks at the general aspect of the object alone and does not believe in the specific aspect as something apart from the general, is called *Samgrahanaya* .[12]

3.*Vyavaharanaya*: That stand point which takes into consideration only the specific properties of an object and maintains that the general is not apart from the specific characteristics ,is *Vyavaharanaya.* [13]

4.*Rjusutranaya:* That stand point which only refers to the present form of an object , without taking into consideration its past and future aspects , is called *Rjusutranaya.* It looks at the natural form of the object present before the mind.[14]

5.*Sabdanaya: Sabdanaya* puts emphasis on the significance of synonymous words having the same sense. As for instance , though the words *Kumbha, Kalasa, ghata* etc. are different in their origins, give the same meaning i.e. the Jar .This is called *Sabdanaya.*[15]

6.*Samabhirudhanaya:* That which holds that with the difference of the words expressing the object, the significance of the object also differs, just as a pot differs from a piece of cloth, so *Kumbha* differs from *Kalasa*, is called S*amabhirudhanaya*[16]

7.*Evambhutanaya:* That standpoint which recognizes an object denoted by a word only when that object is in the actual state of performing its natural function as suggested by the derivative meaning of the word , is called *Evambhutanaya.*[17]

Of these seven kinds of *nayas* , each succeeding stand point is purer than the preceding one. These *nayas* are very important for the understanding of the *Anekantavada* of the Jainas. These *nayas* point to the fact that reality is of various nature , and admits of different descriptions. Any one of these views cannot be taken as the absolute truth.

11. PKM , 6 .74 .
12. Ibid . P .677.
13. Ibid
14. Ibid , P . 678 .
15. Ibid .
16. Ibid ,P . 680 .
17. Ibid .

3.THE DOCTRINE OF SYADVADA:

The theory of *Syadvada* (theory of the assertion of possibilities) is the most important theory propounded by the Jainas to explain the nature of reality. This topic is found in the *Sutra Krtanganiryukti* of Bhadrabahu. It has been developed later on into the *Saptabhanginaya.* (sevenfold judgement)

The Jainas believe that every substance *(dravya)* possesses the characteristics of production , destruction and continuous existence. For instance, a pot is produced from clay and is later destroyed , but clay with its essential characteristics continues to exist in both these states of production and destruction. The Jainas feel that all these assertions of existence , destruction and continuity are true of a thing only under certain conditions. Accordingly it is held that a thing can be represented in innumerable ways or by innumerable determinations referring to different view points, and that for having the full knowledge of an object, one should consider all these aspects. That means for knowing the full nature of a thing , one should take into account not only the positive aspects of the thing but also its negative ones i.e. its distinction from other things.

Hence, it is evident that according to the Jainas the correct description of a thing will be the description of all the aspects of that thing .But the aspects of the thing being infinite in number it is not possible to give a correct description of a thing. "This means that under no circumstances , we can have a predicate which is the only the predicate about a particular subject; any assertion of a thing is sure to be partial, one sided and incomplete." [18] To express this idea the Jainas forward the view of *Syadvada.*

The Jainas use the term '*syat*' meaning 'somehow', only to denote that the jar , for instance, in the expression 'a jar is *sat*' ,exists in its own form , but not in the form of any other thing. By this , they mean that reality being many sided in nature ,vocabulary fails to express a thing in all its aspects, and hence all the assertions are

18.Snha ,K .P. , *The Phiolosophy of Jainism,*. P .11 .

relative , qualified and conditional ; no particular assertion can represent a thing absolutely .This theory is called *Syadvada* as distinct from *Nayavada. Syadvada* is designed to harmonies the different conclusions arrived by the Nayavada.

Syadvada is also called *Saptabhanginaya . Saptabhanginaya* means ' the theory of seven fold judgment.' The seven steps are as follows:

1.*Syadasti*: Somehow , a thing is existent.

2.*Syannasti*: Somehow , a thing is not existent.

3. .*Syadastinasti*: Somehow, a thing is both existent and non existent.

4.*Syadavaktavyam*: Somehow, a thing is indescribable.

5.*Syadasti ca avaktavyam*: Somehow, a thing is both existent and indescribable.

6.*Syadnasti ca avaktavyam* : Somehow, a thing is both non existent and indescribable.

7. *Syadasti ca nasti ca avaktavyam* : Somehow, a thing is existent non existent and indescribable.

This may be further explained in the following way :

1.Somehow, a thing is existent i.e. from a certain point of view of its own material, place, time and nature, it is existent .Thus, a jar is existent in the form of earthly substance, at a particular place , at a particular timeand in a particular form. This is what is meant by *Syadasti.*

2. Somehow , a thing is non existent means from a certain point of view of the material, place , time and nature of another thing, it is non existent. Thus, the Jar does not exist as made of metal, at a different place or time or of a different shape and size. This is what is meant by *Syannasti.*

3. Somehow, a thing is both existent and non existent means from a certain point of view, it is both existent and non existent . Thus, a jar is existent with reference to its own material, place, time and nature , and is non existent with reference to the material, time place and nature of another thing.[19] This is what is meant by *Syadasti nasti.*

19. syat astyeva nastyeva iti kramatah vidhinisedhakalpanaya trtiyah .Hemacandra's Commentory on SM , 23 .

28

4. Somehow, a thing is indescribable means from a certain point of view , it is indescribable , being both existent and non existent at the same time. Thus , a jar is indescribable because it is both existent and non-existent at the same time . That means , existence and non existence being mutuallyexclusive, cannot be simultaneously attributed to one and the same thing at the same time.[20] This is what is meant by *Syadavaktavya.*

5.Somehow, a thing is existent with reference to its own nature and is considered indescribable being both existent and non existent, then it is called *Syadasti ca avaktavyam.*

6. Somehow, a thing is both non existent and indescribable. Thus, a Jar is non existent with reference to the nature of another and is also indescribable. It is called *Syadnasti ca avaktavyam.*

7. Somehow, a thing is both existent , non existent and also indescribable. Thus, a jar is existent with reference to the nature of its own and non existent with reference to the nature of another and is also considered indescribable. This is called *Syadasti ca nasti ca avaktavyam.*

4.THE JAINA CONCEPTION OF SUBSTANCE:

According to the Jaina theories of *Anekantavada* and *Syadvada* , nothing can be said to be possessing a character or characters absolutely. A thing can be described as having different or even opposite characters from different angles of view.

The Jainas hold that there are two kinds of characters found in the every substance. These are essential character and accidental character. The essential characters of a substance remain in the substance as long as the substance remains. Without these the substance cannot exist .For example, consciousness is an essential character of the substance called soul. The accidental characters of a substance come and go. Desires, volitions, pleasure and pain are such accidental characters possessed by the soul substance. It is through such characters that a substance undergoes changes or modifications. There are also called modes. The Jainas use the term *guna*

20.syat avaktavyam iti yugapat vidhinisedhakalpanaya caturthah .Ibid .

to denote the essential unchanging character, and *paryaya*, for an accidental changing character. A substance is defined, therefore, as that which possesses qualities *(gunas)* as well as modes *(paryayas)*.[21]

Accordingly, the Jainas hold that the substance is not merely a permanent entity behind the qualities as is held by the Advaita Vedantins nor is it a chain of momentary existents, as held by the Buddhists. According to them. " substance is that which persists in and through its own qualities and modifications. It is dynamic reality , an identity with changes."[22] It is changing every moment through the *paryayas* or modes or accidental qualities , yet it remains permanent through its *gun* as or essential qualities.[23]

According to Jainas , substance and quality are inseparable. Qualities or *gunas* inhere in substances. Jaina metaphysics does not recognize qualities without substances nor substances without qualities. Qualities without a substratum and a substratum without qualities are both empty abstractions. The Nyaya theory of the absolute distinction between the substance and quality is refuted by the Jainas. A thing exists in and through the qualities and the qualities constitute the thing. The Jainas argue that if the substance is entirely separate and distinct from its qualities, then it may change into infinite substances. Again if the qualities can exist separately from their substance, there will be no necessity for a substance at all.[24] Substance and qualities may be externally related as in "Devadatta's cow" , or internally as in the "all cow" Just as *dhana* and *jnana* (wealth and wisdom) , make the owners *dhani* and *jnani* (rich and wise) , though expressing two ways of relationship , unity and diversity, even so the relation between substance and qualities implies two view of identity and difference.[25] The relation between substance and quality is one of coeval identity , unity, inseparability and essential simplicity.

The substance with the qualities must exist in some form or state. This mode of existence is *paryaya(*mode) and is subject to change. There is a difference between

21.gunaparyayavad dravyam .TAS , 5.38.
22.Vide , *Indian Philosophy* . , vol .1. , P.260.
23. Vide , *The philosophy of Jainism* , P. 40 .
24. Vide , *Indian Philosophy* . , vol .1. , P.260.
25.Ibid

quality and a mode. Yellowness, hardness and brightness are said to be qualities of gold. With this gold a necklace can be made and bangles can be made and they are the various modified form of gold. The *gunas* or qualities continue while the *prayayas* or modifications change.[26]

A substances is real (*sat*). There are three factors present in reality, namely, permanence, origination and decay .In a substance there is its unchanging essence and so it is permanent .There are again the origin and decay of its changing modes(*paryaya*). Hence all the three elements that characterize reality are there in a substance.

5.CLASSIFICATION OF SUBSTANCE:

Substances are broadly divided into two classes viz. extended (*astikaya*) and non extended (*anastikaya*).There is only one substance , namely, time *(kala)*, which is devoid of extension .All other substances possess extension. So, the extended substances are called by the general name *astikaya* because every substance of this kind exists (*asti*) like a body (*kaya*) , possessing extension.

The whole universe is brought under the two everlasting, uncreated, eternal and co-existing things which are called living (*Jiva*) and non living (*ajiva*) . The *jiva* is the enjoyer and the *ajiva* is the enjoyed. *Jiva* means the conscious spirit and *ajiva* means the unconscious non- spirit. *Ajiva* includes matter which is called *pudgala*, space , motion , rest and time .[27] Thus , the *asitkaya* substances are sub divided into five classes ,viz., *jiva*(soul), *pudgala* (matter) , *akasha*(space) , *dharma*(motion) , and *adharma(*rest) . These are technically called *pancastikaya* which possess constituent parts extending in space. Again *Kala* (time) is the only *anastikaya dravya* which has no extension in space . If *kala* (time) is added to this five *astikayas* , then we have the six dravyas of Jaina metaphysics .According to some , categories are of seven types , viz. , *jiva* , *ajiva* , *asrava* , *bandha* , *samvara* , *nirjara* and *moksa* .Some others , again add two more types , viz. , *papa* and *punya* and regard categories as of nine kinds .

26. Ibid ., P .261 .
27.bodhatmako jivah .abodhatmakastvajivah .SDS , P.67.
    apare punarjivajivayoraparam prapancamacaksate
    jivakasadharmadharmapudgalastikayabhedat .Ibid . , P.69.

6.AJIVA OR THE INANIMATE SUBSTANCES.

The Ajiva or inanimate substances is divided into two main classes . These are arupin and rupin .Arupin or those are without form are *dharma , adharma ,* space , time , and rupin or those with form are *pudgala* or matter.

(i) Pudgala : In Jaina philosophy , matter is called *pudgala ,* because its extent is sometimes increased on account of the combination of its parts(*pud* = to combine or to increase) and is sometimes decreased as a result of their dissociation (*gala* = to dissociate or to decrease .[28] Material substances can combine together to form larger and larger wholes , and can also break up into smaller and smaller parts .The smallest parts of matter which can not be further divided , being partless is called atoms (*anu)* . Two or more such atoms may combine together to form compounds . Our bodies and the objects of nature are such compounds of material atoms .Mind , speech and breath are also the products of matter .[29]

Being an *ajiva* or unconscious substance , *pudgala* is different from the self , the conscious principle and similar to the principles of motion (*dharma*) rest (*adharma*) , space (*akasa)* and time (*kala*) . On the other hand , matter is similar to the self, since both are conceived by the Jainas to be active principles and to have forms or *murta* , while the other four substances are inactive and *amurta* or formless .[30] Kundakunda defines *pudgala* as that which can be experienced by the five sense organs . The five sense –organs , the five varieties of body , namely , *audsarika , vaikriyaka , aharaka , taijasa* and *karmana* , means , the karmic matter and all *murtas* are made of *pudgalas.*[31]

According to the Jainas , matter plays an important role in the progress of the self . The bondage of the self is caused by its contact with matter and attain liberation as a result of its dissociation from it . The other four unconscious substances are

---

28. puranad galanad api pudgalanam svabhavajnaih kathyate pudgalah .
    Tattvarthasara , 3.55.
29.Vide , *Introduction to Indian Philosophy* , P.96.
30.akasakalajiva dharmadharmau ca murtiparihinah *I*
   *m*urtam pudgaladravyam jivah khalu cetanas tesu *II* PKS , 97 .
31. Ibid ., 82 .

absolutely passive principles which have nothing to do with the bondage and liberation of the self .

A *pudgala* possesses the four qualities of touch , taste , smell and colour.[32] These qualities are possessed by atoms and also by their products , the compounds. Like these four , sound is not an original quality. The Jainas point out that sound along with light , heat , shadow , darkeness , union, disunion, fineness, grossness , shape is produced later by the accidental modifications of matter .[33T] The four qualities touch , taste, smell and colour are sub –divided into manifold. Touch is eightfold such as hard, soft, heavy, light, cold, hot, smooth and rough .Taste is five fold, viz., bitter, pungent, acrid, sour and sweet . Smell is of two types, fragrant and bad ; and colour is five fold :dark, white, blue, yellow, and red .

According to the *Pancastikayasamaya-sara* , there are four modes or states of *pudgala* , namely , *skandha* , *skandhapradesa* , *skandhadesa* , and *paramanu.* *Skandha* is matter in its gross form , which is formed by aggregate of *paramanus* or primary atoms . *Skandhadesa* is described as a part of *skandha* . *Skandhapradesa* as an unseparated minute part of *Skandhadesa* .*Paramanu* is the ultimately separated minutest part of *pudgala* .Thus while *skandha* is a complete molecular constitution , *skandhadesa* and *skandhpradesa* are incomplete masses . Of these four modes of matter , *skandha* , *skandhadesa* and *skandhpradesa* may be denoted by the term '*skandha*' and accordingly , *pudgala* may be said to have two forms *paramanu* or atom and *skandha* or aggregate of atoms .[34]

Pudgala , principally means the *paramanus* or primary atoms , but the term is applied to the *skandas* also .[35] Amrtacandra Suri says that *paramanus* are called *pudgalas* , as they possess the qualities of combination and dissociation. *Skandhas* are

32.sparsarasagandhavarnavantah pudgalah . SDS , P .71 .
33.TAS , 5.24.
34.skandhas ca skandhadesah *I*
  skandhapradesas ca bhavanti paramanavah *II*
  skandhah sakalasamastas tasya tvardham bhananti desa iti *I*
  ardhardham ca pradesah paramanus caivavibhagi *II* PKS , 74-75 .
  anavah skandhas ca . TAS , 5.25.
35.cf , PKS , 76 .

also *pudgalas* , since they are the combinations or modifications of several *pudgalas* [36]

The Jainas say that colour , smell , taste , and touch are the special qualities of *tejas* , *prthivi* , *ap* ,and *vayu* respectively .But in the ultimate analysis , the Jainas deny the qualitative difference among the atoms . According to them , the primary matter is of one kind only , which contains the potentiality to manifest the qualities in the gross material bodies.[37]

(ii).*Akasa* : Etymologically the word *akasa* may mean three things (i) That in which all things are revealed , (ii) That which is self revealing .(iii) That which gives *Avakasa* or space to all things .[38] The Jainas accept only the third meaning of the word *akasa* . *Avakasa* or the characteristic of giving space to substance is explained by a reference to the act of *avagaha* or entering into space by other substances . *Akasa* allows *avakasa* or space to all things entering into it ; and all things have *avagaha* or entrance into space . In other words , it is that in which all other principles , namely , soul , matter , time , motion , and rest find their abode . [39] The Jainas illustrate *avakasa* and *avagahana* by saying that while a swan enters into the water of a pond, the swan has *avagahana* into the water and the water gives *avakasa* to the swan .In the same way , there is *avagahana* of all other things into *akasa* and *akasa* gives them *avakasa* or accommodation .[40] This does not mean that *akasa* actively gives accommodation or *avakasa* to other realities .Actually all other realities get accommodation in *akasa* because of their expanse .Being an inactive substance *akasa* does not come forward actively to give accommodation to other realities . This passive function performed by *akasa* is technically called by the Jainas as baladhana , which is opposed to active causation.[41] The Jainas hold that all things have the capacity to occupy some space . This implies that there is some entity which

36. Vide , *The Philosophy of Jainism* , P. 52 .
37.Ibid .,
38.Vide. , *Reals in the Jaina Metaphysics* ,P.31 .
39.akasasyavagahah . TAS , 5.18.
   Yad dadati vivaramakhilam talloke bhavatyakasam . PKS , 90 .
40. Vide , *The Philosophy of Jainism* , P. 53 .
41.cf . kryahetutvam etesam niskryanam na hiyate *I*
   yatah khalu baladhanamatramatra vivaksitam *II* Tattvarthasara ,2.39.

34

serves as the common ground in which all things exist that common ground is *akasa* .*Akasa* is not a material substance , it is mere extension .

Akasa is infinite , eternal , and formless . Its pradesas or subtle parts are said to be infinite in number . The smallest part of *akasa* is called *akasanu* or space –atom . Each *akasanu* has the capacity to give space to one smallest particle of each of the categories of *jiva , pudgala , kala , dharma ,* and *adharma* .[42]

Acording to the Jainas , *akasa* consists of two parts-*loka* and *aloka* .The space containing the world where souls and the other substances live is called *lokakasa* .And empty space beyond such world is called *alokakasa* .[43]

(iii).Kala: Umasvami states that time makes possible the continuity , modification , movement , newness and oldness of substances .[44] Time is inferred , though not perceived . Without time a thing can not continue to exist . Duration implies moments of time in which existence is prolonged Without time modification or change of states also can not be conceived . A mango can be green and ripe only at different moments of time Movement which implies the assumption of successive states by an object can be conceived only with the supposition of time . Simalarly . the distinction between the old and the new , the earlier and the later cannot be explained without time . Therefore , these are the grounds on which the existence of time can be inferred . *Kala* has two aspects- *vyavaharika kala* or phenomenal time and *paramarthika kala* or noumenal time . Continuty or duration *(vartana)* is the mark of noumenal time . The phenomenal time is conventionally divided into different parts, such as moments , hours , days , months etc. and is limited by a beginning and an end . But noumenal time is formless and eternal .By imposing conventional limitations and distinctions on noumenal time , phenomenal time is produced .[45] Gunaratna again points out that some Jaina teachers do not admit time as a separate substance , but regard it as a mode of the other substances.[46]

42. Vide , *The philosophy of Jainism* , P. 53 .
43. lokakasam alokakasam iti dvidham .
   BDS, as quoted in *The Philosophy of Jainism*, P. 53
44.vartana-parinama-kryah paratvaparatve ca kalasya . TAS , 5.22.
45.BDS ,21.
46. Vide , *An Introduction to Indian Philosophy*, P.98 .

(iv).*Dharma*: In the Jaina system, *dharma* is a non-material entity. It is described as the cause of motion (*gatikaranam*). It is non-material , as it is devoid of the qualites of smell , taste , colour etc. which are the attributes of matter.It is non –psychical ,since it is non conscious .Like *kala , akasa* or space , *dharma* is also formless and inactive .It is said to pervade the whole of the *lokakasa* and conditions the movement of the *pudgalas* and the selves. It has innumerable *pradesas* or parts , yet it is a continuous and extended whole , i. e. an indivisible single substance , since its parts are inseparable .[47]

The definition , however , of *dharma* as the *gatikaranam* does not mean that it moves the things .*Dharma* is clearly stated to be a *niskrya* or inactive substance .It is simply a *bahiranga-hetu* (external) or *udasina-hetu* (indifferent cause) of the motions of things .Matreial things and the selves move by themselves ; *dharma* simply assists them passively in this act of moving .Kundakanda and Nemicandra say that *dharma* simply helps the movement of the moving matter or soul , just as water helps the movement of a fish ; it does not move the non-moving.[48]

The principle of dharma is without any form and is devoid of taste , colour , sound , and touch . It exists in the *lokakasa* , but not in *alokakasa* or the infinite void space lying beyond *lokakasa* .This is the reason why the emancipated soul, although it has the inherent nature of moving upwards , stops at the top of *lokakasa* and can not move into *alokakasa* .This existence of dharma is a mark which distinguishes *lokakasa* from *alokakasa* .[49] *Dharma* is of three kinds , *skandha, desa* and *pradesa* . *Dharma* as a whole of *skandha* , a large fraction of *skandha* is *desa* ; and a small fraction of *desa* is *pradesa* .[50]

47.dharmastikayo'raso'varnagandho'sabdo'sparsah. *I*
   lokavagarhah sprstah prthulo'samkhyatapradesah *II* PKS ,83.
   gatikryayuktanam karanabhutah .Ibid . , 84.
48.gatiparinatanam dharmah pudgalajivanam gamanasahakari *I*
   toyam yatha matsyanam agacchatam naiva sa nayati *II* BDS ,17.
   na ca gacchati dharmastiko gamanam na karotyanyadravyasya *I*
   bhavati gatis prasaro jivanam pudgalanam ca *II* PKS ,88
49. Vide , *The philosophy of Jainism* , P. 56 .
50. Ibid .

(v).Adharma : Like *dharma* , *adharma* is also a non-physical and non-psychical eternal entity . It is non- physical , as it is devoid of the qualities of touch , taste , smell etc. It is non –psychical , since it is devoid of consciousness .Like , *kala , akasa* , and *dharma* , it is also formless and inactive . It pervades the entire *lokakasa* and conditions the rest of stoppage of the *pudgalas* and the selves. It has innumerable *pradesa* or parts , but yet it is an indivisible single substance or a continuous and extended whole , as its parts are inseparable .[51]

Adharma is described as *sthitikaranam* or the cause of the rest ,
since it is the principle which determines the rest or inaction of the *pudgalas* and the selves .[52] Though *adharma* is said to be the cause of rest , it does not mean that *adharma* is an active principles stopping substances in motion . It is a *niskrya* or inactive principles . It is simply a *bahirangahetu* (external) or *udasinahetu* (indifferent cause) of the inactivities of things .The material things and the selves stop by themselves ; *adharma* simply assists them passively in this act resting or stopping .[53] Like *dharma, kala, pudgala* and the *Jiva, adharma* also exists only in the *lokakasa* and does not extend to the *anantakasa* or the empty infinite space lying beyond *lokakasa.*

Again, like *dharma* , *adharma* is also of three kinds- *skandha, desa* and *pradesa* . *Adharma* as the whole is *skandha,* a large fraction of *skandha* is *desa* ; and a small fraction of *desa* is *pradesa* .

51.yatha bhavati dharmadravyam tatha tajjanihi dravyam adharmakhyam .PKS ,86.
52.sthitikryayuktam karanabhutam tu prthiviva . Ibid .,86.
  sthanayuktanam adharmah pudgalajivanam sthanasahakari .BDS ,18.
53. Vide , *The Philosophy of Jainism* , P. 57 .

CHAPTER – III
JAINA CONCEPT OF THE SELF

1.THE CONCEPT OF SELF IN OTHER SYSTEMS :

Self or soul is an important topic of discussion in Indian philosophy. Almost all the systems of Indian philosophy admit the existence of a permanent entity, which is variously called *atman, purusa* or *jiva*. Regarding the real nature of the self, however there are great controversies among the philosophers . Among the *nastika* schools, the Carvaka rejects the reality of the self and identifies it with the body endowed with consciousness .[1] The Buddhist denies the reality of the permanent self and regards it as a series of momentary ideas .[2] Only the Jainas admits the reality of the permanent self as a knowing , feeling and active agent . All the *astika* schools of Indian Philosophy admit the existence of the self or *atman* as a permanent spiritual substance . The Nyaya and the Vaisesika regard the self as an eternal substance endowed with cognition , pleasure , pain , desire , aversion , volition , impression , merit and demerit . It acquires consciousness in conjunction with the body and the eternal organ .[3] The Samkhya and the Yoga regard the self or *purusa* as an eternal spirit whose essence is consciousness .[4] The Advaita Vedanta admits the reality of one self , which is pure being , pure consciousness and pure bliss , and identifies it with *Brahman* .[5] The Mimamsa regard the self as an eternal substance .[6] Kumarila regards knowledge as a mode or activity of the self while Prabhakara regards it as a quality of the self .

All the systems of Indian philosophy which accept the existence of the self maintain that the self is pure and unsullied in its nature and all impurities of action or

1.caitanyavisistadeha eva atma .SDS , P.3.
2.sarrvam ksanikam ksanikam Ibid , P.19.
3.atmatvasamanyavanatma sukhadukhadivaicitryat pratisariram bhinnah .TBh, P. 189.
4.trigunamaviveki visayah samanyamacetanampra savadharmi *I*
  vyaktam tatha pradhanam tadviparitastatha ca puman *II* SK , 11 .
5. atna ca brahma .BSSB , 1.1.1.
6.Vide , *A critical Survey of Indian Philosophy* ,P .234 .

passion do not form a real part of it . The ultimate end of human life is attained when all impurities are removed and the pure nature of the self is clearly apprehended and all other extraneous connections with it are absolutely disassociated .

A. THE SELF IN NYAYA –VAISESIKA PHILOSOPHY :

Both the Nyaya and the Vaisesika systems are realistic and pluralistic . These systems hold that all the objects of the world have ontological reality , and every object is different from every other object . Both the systems accept the self as a substance and every self is different from every other self as well as every other category .

According to the Nyaya and the Vaisesika , the self is of two types, viz., *jivatman* or the individual self and *paramatman* or the supreme self or God . The *jivatman* is infinite in number and is different in every individual , while *paramatman* is only one . [7] The term *atman* is used to denote both the individual self and *paramatman* or God . *Atman* means the locus of knowledge and both the self and God share this nature .[8] *Atman* is that which is the substance of *iccha* or will and *prayatna* or volition . The self is a real and incorporeal substance . It is *niravayava* or partless and *nitya* or eternal . Being an unchangeable and imperishable substance , the self is not subject to origination and destruction . The self is all pervasive in magnitude .[9] It cannot be atomic . If the self were atomic , it would not be perceived .Moreover if the self were atomic, it would not be possible for its cognition to extend all over the body . Further if the self were smaller than the body, it could not occupy the whole body as it actually does ; if it larger than the body , the latter could not contain the former ; and if it were equal to the size of the body , then either it could be too small for the body which grows day by day or it would be endowed with growth and development like the body .[10]

7.sa dvidah-jivatma paramatma ca . tatra isvarah sarvajnah paramatmaika eka
   sukhaduhkhadirahitah .jivatma pratisariram bhinnah TS , P. 7.
8.jnanadhikaranamatma .Ibid .
9. vibhurnityasca .Ibid .
10.sa ca na paramanu parimanah sarira vyapisukhadyanupalabdhiprasangat .
   na madhyama parimanah tatha sati anityatvaprasangena ,
   krtanasakrtabhyagamprasangat. tasmannityo vibhurjivah .Ibid . , P.8 .

Thus the self is all-pervasive and not located in a particular body and exists in all space . But though the self is all pervading , its actions and feelings are perceived only in a particular body .

According to the Nyaya-Vaisesika, then self is different from the body, the sense organs, the mind and intellect. The body can not be regarded as the self, because the quality of consciousness can not reside in the body . Thus, in the states of death and trance , consciousness is not experienced though the body exists .[11] If the body be the self, then the body being subject to incessant change, the self also will have to be regarded as an everchanging substance . In that case, all moral values will become meaningless, since there will be no persisting self to experience the effect of its actions .[12] Similarly, the sense-organs also can not be the self because consciousness can not exist in the senses . Moreover , the senses can not control themselves , nor can they synthesis their experiences . Therefore , there must be some other agent , i.e. the self , to control them and synthesis their experiences .[13] Neither can the mind be regarded as the self . For being an internal instrument of knowledge , the mind also requires to be controlled by some agent . Further if the mind were the self , its quality of consciousness could not be perceived , since the mind is atomic in magnitude , and the qualities of atomic substances are imperceptible .[14] This permanent self is not *buddhi* or intellection , *upalabdhi* or apprehension , or *jnana* or knowledge . *Buddhi* is non-permanent , while the soul must be permanent .[15] Thus the self must be quite different from all other substances .

Both the Nyaya and the Vaisesika systems have maintained that the selves are many . Both being realistic systems believe in spiritual pluarilism . The self is unique in each individual . Hence , it is infinite in number . They argue that if there were only one self in all the individuals, then every body would share the feelings , thoughts , actions etc. of all other individual , which is not tenable . Hence , the self

11.sairasya na caitanyam mrtesu vyabhicaratah .BP, 48 .
12.cf. . *Nyayasiddantamuktavali* on Ibid
13.cf. atmendriyadhyadhisthata karanam hi sakartrkam .BP., 47.
14.mano'pi na tatha jnanadyanadhyaks dam tada bhavet .Ibid. , 49.
15.Radhakrishnan ,S., *Indian Philosophy* , Vol. ii , P.130.

must be regarded as different in each organism .[16]

In empirical state , the self is endowed with the body, sense-organs, vital airs , mind and so on , though it is different from all these elements . By the influence of ignorance and the merits and demerits accruing from the past actions or *karmanas* , the self is endowed with a real ego or *ahamkara* and undergoes bondage . As a result , it is attached to the objects of enjoyment , and acts for attainment of pleasure and avoidance of pain . Such an empirical self is a real knower , doer and enjoyer and is endowed with the qualities of desire , aversion . volition , pleasure , pain , cognition etc .[17]

However in the state of liberation , the self is not affected by ignorance and the merits and demerits ;and it realizes its real nature . Then the self is unaffected by attachment , desire , aversion , volition , feelings etc . Which are all connected with the body and the mind .In liberation , the self is a pure substance divested not only of pains and ignorance but also of pleasure and consciousness .[18]

B.THE SELF IN SAMKHYA- YOGA PHILOSOPHY :

Both the Samkhya and the Yoga philosophy are pluralistics . Both the systems accept twentyfive principles .Of them twentyfive , *Purusa* and *prakrti* are the ultimate realities . The Samkhya and the Yoga philosophy regards the *purusa* , which is nothing but the self as a spiritual entity .Patanjali describes *purusa* as *drasta* or seer . It is the power of consciousness or knowledge which is the nature of *purusa* .[19] It is neutral ; it has neither any attachment nor any aversion to anything . It is inactive but conscious and hence it is different from *prakrti* which is active and unconscious . According to Isvarakrisna *purusa* is unchangeable and immutable . It is eternal in the sense that it is not affected by the change of time, and that it is not an uncaused ultimate principle. It is independent and is not supported by anything else . The *purusa* is the nature of pure consciousness . It is the ultimate knower which is the

16. cf. *Nyayadarsanavimarsah* , P.33 .
17. BP., 23 &24 .
18. cf. *Nyayadarsanavimarsah* , P.35 .
19.drsta drsimatrah suddho'pi pratyayanupasyah .YS , 2.20.
    drsimatra iti , drksaktireva visesanaparamrstetyarthah .YBh ,on Ibid .

foundation of all knowledge . It is the pure subject and as such can never become an object of knowledge . It is the silent witness , the emancipated alone , the peaceful eternal .It is the self –luminous and self –proved . It is uncaused , eternal and all-pervading . It is called *nistraigunya* , *udasina* , *akarta* , *kevala* , *madhyastha* , *saksi* , *drasta* , *sadaprakashasvarupa* and *jnata* [20] *Purusa* or the self is different from all the elements of the world of objects. It is different from matter or the material body , the senses , the mind and the intellect .*Purusa* is different from matter , because the latter is the known , while the former is the knower . It is different from the senses since the senses are the instruments of knowing , while the self is the knower itself .It is different from the mind because the mind is active and composed of *gunas* . *Purusa* is different from *buddhi* or the intellect , since the latter is unconscious , but the former is conscious .[21]

Though the *purusa* is different from the body , senses , mind and intellect , but in the empirical state , it is neither quite similar to these elements nor quite distinct from them .[22]

In empirical state *purusa* or the self wrongly identifies itself with the mental modes which assumes the forms of objects and in which the *purusa* is reflected .Hence *Pancasika* , as quoted in the *Vyasa-bhasya* , says , " Not knowing the *purusa* beyond the time to be different there from in nature , character , Knowledge etc , a man has the notion of self in the mind through delusion . [23] The bondage and subsequent release of the self only refer to the self as reflected in *buddhi* . The self , which realizes its distinction from its reflection , is said to be free . Hence , liberation here means , the realization of the real nature of the self .[24] The Samkhya Yoga

20.tasmacca viparyasatsiddham saksitvamasya purusasya *I*
    kaivalyam madhyasthyam drstrtvamakartrbhavasca *II* SK ,19. STK on it .
21.sariradivyatiriktah puman .SS , 1. 139 .
    dehadivyatirikto'sau vaicitryat .Ibid , 6.2.
22.sa buddherna sarupo natyantam virupa iti .YBh , 2.20.
23.bhoktrbhogy   asaktyaratyantavibhaktayor------------
    buddhitah   param   purusamakara ------------
    kuryattatratmabuddhim   mohena iti .Ibid ,2.6.
24.tada drstuh svarupe'vasthanam.YS , 1.3.
    kaivalyam svarupapratistha va citisaktiriti . Ibid ,4.34.

philosophers maintain the plurality of selves not only in the empirical state but transcendental level also .In Yoga philosophy , *Isvara* or God is regarded as a particular self . Patanjanli defines *Isvara* as a special kind of *purusa* untouched by afflictions , actions , effects and dispositions .[25] The relation between *Isvara* and the *purusa* is not inseparable .*Purusas* are eternally existing and all pervading realities . They do not come out of *Isvara* and are not dissolved into Him in liberation .A spiritual aspirant attains liberation by the acquisition of mental equilibrium . The meditation on *Isvara* is simply one of the means for attaining this mental equilibrium . *Isvara* in Yoga philosophy is said to help the devotees indirectly by removing the obstacles standing in the way of their spiritual progress .[26] According to Vacaspati Misra and Vijnana Bhiksu , *"Isvara* helps the *purusa* attain their ends , by guiding *prakriti* in suitable direction ."[27] But the self is not required to aspire for union with *Isvara* .

C.THE SELF IN ADVAITA VEDANTA PHILOSOPHY :

The Advaita Vedanta of Sankara regards *Brahman* as the ultimate reality .There is no distinction between the Self and *Brahman* . The Advaita Vedantin hold that though the differenceless *Brahman* is the only reality , it appears as the empirical selves and the manifold world through *maya* , otherwise called *ajnana* or *avidya* .The entire Vedanta philosophy may be summarized in a line –"*Brahman* is true , the world is false and the *jiva* and Brahman are not not different ." [28]

The Advaita Vedantin holds that the self or *atman* is identical with *Brahman* . It is the highest transcendental reality . It is Brahman itself .[29] The *atmon* is of the nature of pure consciousness . Pure consciousness is identical with the existence and bliss . The conception of existence involves the idea of truth , immutability and completeness . Thus the real self is unconditionally true , eternal , unchangeable and

25.klesakarmavipakasayairaparamrstah purusavisesa isvarah . YS ,1.24.
26.isvarapranidhanadva . Ibid ,1.23.
 pranidhanad bhaktivisesadavarjita isvarastamanugrhatyabhidhyanamatrena .
 YBh , on ibid .
27.Vide , *Outlines of Indian Philosophy* , PP.297-298.
28.brahma satyam jagannithya jivo brahmaiva naparah .
 Quoted in Sanskrtnibandhasatakam , P.56 .
29.atma ca brahma . BSSB , 1.1.1.

Self complete . It is not subjected to bondage and suffering , because it is of the nature of pure knowledge and bliss .[30] It is omnipresent , universal and infinite because consciousness is without any limitation . The *atman* is all pervasive and not conditioned by time and space . It is neither atomic nor intermediary in size . The self or atman is one and the same self exists in all beings. It is ever shining .As the sun shines when there is nothing to shine , so the conscious self shines even when there is no object .[31] *Atman* is without any quality ; the qualities that seem to pertain to the self are only apparent . It is devoid of action , because action involves an idea of change in the subject , while *atman* is changeless . [32]

According to the Advaita Vedanta , the self conditioned either by *avidya* or by the *antahkarana* i.e. the internal organ is revealed as the *jiva* or empirical self .In other word , *atman* or the transcendental , metaphysical self appears as the *jiva* or the empirical , phenomenal self due to *avidya* . It is this empirical self or *jiva* that performs actions , enjoys their fruits and undergoes birth and rebirth .

The *jiva* is in essence one with *Brahman* .[33] Though the self is pure , it seems to be subject to the worldly defects because of *avidya* .Sankara distinguishes carefully the self that is implied in all experience from the self which is an observed fact of introspection , the metaphysical subject or the " I " and the psychological subject or the " me " . While the Atman is purely cognitive , one individual consciousness is essentially an active striving towards some end . [34] he *Jiva* is the knower ,doer and enjoyer .[35] It acquires merits and demerits according to its good and bad deeds and experiences their fruits . It is subject to transmigration and bondage . Though the *jiva* is non-different from *Brahman* and is one without a second , yet it is regarded as many or different in different individuals due to the limiting adjunct .[36] The limiting adjunct is the mind body complex which is the effect of *ajnana* .

30. purusa hi vinasahetvabhavat vikriyahetvabhavacca kutastha nityah , atu eva nityasuddabuddhamuktasvabhavah . Ibid , 1.1.4.
31.Ibid . , 2.3.18.
32. Ibid . , 1.3.24.
33.tattvamasi ayamatma brahma .CU , 6.8.7.
34. Radhakrishnan ,S., *Indian Philosophy* , Vol. ii , P.595.
35.BSSB ,1.3.40.
36.bhedastu upadhinimitto mithyajnananakalpito na paramarthikah .Ibid .,1.4.10.

There is again difference of opinion among the Advaita Vedantins regarding the number of the *jiva* . Most of them hold that there are many *jivas* because the adjunct of the *jiva* is different in different individuals. They also hold that multiplicity of the *jivas* must be maintained in order to distinguish between the bound and the released *jivas.* [37] On the other hand , some Advaita Vedantins , like the upholders of *Drsti-srsti-vada* , maintain that the *jiva* is not many but one ; other *jivas* as well as their bondage and liberation are illusory creation of the single Jiva .[38]

The later Vedantins accept an intermediate stage called *saksin* or witness self in between the *jiva* and the *atman* . This *saksin* is different from both of them . According to the author of *Vedantaparibhasa* , the *saksin* is the eternal consciousness conditioned by the internal organ .A *jiva* is the eternal consciousness limited by the internal organ .The internal organ is here a qualification which enters into the being of eternal consciousness.[39]

2. THE SELF OR JIVA IN JAINA PHILOSOPHY :

In Jaina philosophy , the term *Jiva* is used in the sense of the self or *atman* . The idea of the *jiva* has occupied an important position in Jaina Philosophy .Jainism aims at the liberation of the *jiva* from the cycle of births and deaths .The Jaina system maintains that the self is a life-principle and is different from the body . The principle of life is entirely distinct from the body ; and it is most erroneous to think that life is either the product or the property of the body .It is on account of this life principle that the body appears to be living . This principle is the self . [40]   This system also maintains that the self is directly perceived . By introspection , anybody can perceive the self . The *jiva* is different from the *ajiva* . *Ajiva* means both material and immaterial or *amutra* entities . Immaterial or *amurta* entities are , space , time , *dharma* and *adharma* , while the material or *murta* entity is the *pudgala* .These entities are different from the self .

37.jivabhedas tavat avasyikah , baddha mukta-pratibhasat . Balabodhini on VS ,36.
38.ekasya eva jivatvat itaresam taddrstivijrmbhitatvena tatah vidvanmanjari on Ibid .
39.jivo nama'ntahkaranavacchinnam caitanyam .
   tatsaksi tu antahkaranopahitam caitanyam VP, P.85.
40.Dasgupta , S.N. , *A History of Indian Philosophy* , P.188.

The thinkers of the Jainism has described the nature of the *jiva* in different ways . According to Kundakundacarya , the *jiva* is existent ; is conscious ; has cognition ; is a doer ; is active ; is an enjoyer ; is of the same size as its body ; is formless ; is attached to *karma* or non psychical matter .[41] Acarya Nemicandra has also said , " *jiva* is possessed of cognition ; is formless ; is a doer ; is of the same extent as its body ; is an enjoyer ; migrates in the *samsara* or in the series of existences ; but is free in its essence ; and has an upward motion ." [42] Vadideva also points out that the *jiva* is essentially conscious ; undergoes modifications ; is a doer ; is a direct enjoyer ; is of the same extent , as its body ; is different in each individual ; has transmigrations owing to its being attached to *Pudgala* or Matter .[43] Hence , according to the Jainas , the most important quality of the self is consciousness .

The Jainas , further hold that consciousness is both the essence and the quality of the self. That means consciousness is not its accidental quality , but it constitutes its essence .[44] Accordingly , the self and consciousness are both identical with and different from each other .[45]

Consciousness is an essential attribute of the self . It is always present in the self , though its nature and degree may very . The consciousness of the self has two manifestations , viz. , *darsana* or vision and *jnana* or knowledge , which are jointly called *upayoga* .[46] *Darsana* is the knowledge of things without their details , while *jnana* means the knowledge of details .The Jainas therefore uphold that *upayoga* is the essential characteristics of the self .[47]

The word *upayoga* may be explained in different ways : Firstly , the word *upa* means 'close ' and *yoga* means 'relation' and hence the word means "that which is closely related to the self ." [48]Secondly , *upayoga* is that by which some function is

41.PKS ,27.
42. BDS ,2.
43.Vide , *Reals in the Jaina Metaphysics* ,P.269.
44.caitanya laksanam jivah .SDSm, 49.
45.jnanadbhinno na nabhinno bhinnabhinnah katamcana .SDS ,P.69
46.jnanadarsane upayogah .Ibid, p.67.
47.upayoga loksnam .TAS ,2.8.
48. Vide , *The Philosophy of Jainism* , P. 84 .

served --- *upayujyate anena iti upayogah* .Thirdly , it is the employment of self's activities .Fourthly , it is the *vyapara* or function of the self . Hence it can be said that *upayoga* is the function of the self . through which it manifests its nature . The self is of the nature of *caitanya* i. e. consciousness . consciousness is revealed as *jnana* and *darsana* i.e. as *upayoga* . This means that *upayoga* is the effect of consciousness .[49] Thus, *upayoga* is the resultant of consciousness ; it is the function or action through which the self or consciousness manifests itself .

There are again some Jaina philosophers who are of the view that *Upayoga* is not the resultant of consciousness . They hold that *upayoga* is the drive which leads to the apprehension of objects .It gives rise to the experience of objects ,and the experience express s itself in the form of *jnana* and *darsana* .[50] But this view is not accepted by the majority of the Jaina Philosophers .In their view , *jnana* and *darsana* are regarded as *upayoga* .[51] Moreover , they regard consciousness as the essence of the *jiva* , and not the effect of *upayoga* .

The Jainas also say that the real nature of the self can be realized through *upayoga* . The self possesses innumerable parts .In the state of bondage , these parts get intermixed with the *karmaparamanus* . *Karmaparamanus* are the atomic particles attracted by the self from outside through its activities . As a result , the self identifies itself with the *karma* particles and can not realize the difference between its own parts and these particles .By knowing the nature of *jnana* and *darsana* , one can know the distinction between the *Karmaparamanus* and the parts of the self .In the other words , it is through *upayoga* that can realize the nature of the self .[52]

The two aspects of *upayoga* are *jnana* and *darsana* . It is said in *Pancastikayasara* that *jnana* and *darsana* are distinguished only from the phenomenal point of view , while in reality they are inseparable .[53] According to the

49. Ibid,
50.cf. ibid.
51.sahajacidrupaparinatim svikurvane jnanadarsane upayogah .SDS ,P.67.
52.sa parasparapradesanam
   pradesabandhatkarmanaikibhutasyatmano'nyatvapratipattikaranam bhavati .Ibid .,
   PP.67-68.
53.PKS ,41.

47

Jainas, *jnana* is neither completely different nor completely identical with the self, but is somehow different and somehow identical with it . *Jnana* being a state of consciousness or the self , is not quite distinct fron the self ,and being a quality of the self , is not quite identical with it . If *jnana* and the self were completely identical , the self would have been described as *jnana* . But *jnana* means "the knowledge of the self ." Hence, the Jainas say that *jnana* must be regarded as *bhinnabhinna* i.e. both different and non different from the self .[54]

Upayoga may be both *suddha* or pure and *asuddha* or impure . *Suddhopayoga* is of the nature of *kevala jnana* and *kevala darsana* , and is manifested in the perfect or liberated beings . *Asuddhopayoga* is of the nature of *mati ,sruta , avadhi* and *manah paryaya* .[55] It is manifested in the imperfect or bound selves . The Jaina say that consciousness is manifested in three ways : viz. *jnanacetana , karmacetana* and *karmaphalacetana* . Of these *jnanacetana* is of the nature of *kevala-jnana* which is associated with the perfect or liberated self . *Karmacetana* is the experience of *karman* . It is manifested in the attachment for something and the detachment from another . The realization of the fruits of *karman* like the feelings of pleasure , pain etc.is called *karmaphalacetana* . *karmacetana* and *karmaphalacetana* are related to the imperfect or bound selves.[56]

According to the Jainas , the self is naturally pure, free , perfect and divine and is endowed with *ananta-catustaya* , i. e. four infinite qualities : *anantadarsana* (infinite vision) , *anantajnana* (infinite knowledge) , *ananta sukha* (infinite-bliss) and *anantavirya* (infinite power) . During the empirical state , its real nature is obscured and enveloped by some atomic particles called *karmaparamanus* or karmic atoms .

The *Jiva* is described from two points of view : the noumenal or *niscayanaya* and the phenomenal or *vyavaharanaya* .From the noumenal point of view , the self is described in the pure form . The phenomenal point of view ascribes the empirical

54.jnanadbhinno na nabhinno bhinnabhinnah katamcana *I*
   jnanam purvaparibhutam so'yamatmeti kirtitah *II* SDS, P.69.
55.sakalavimalakevala jnanadars'anadravyam suddhopayogah *I*
   matijnanadirupah vikalah asuddhopayogah *II* BDS ,15.
56.cf.karmanam phalam ekah ekah karyam tu jnanam arthaikah *I*
   cetayati jivarasis cetakabhavena trividhena .PKS ,38.

qualities to the self .[57]

According to the Jainas , the self is always subject to change or modification .During the state of bondage , it undergoes changes by the influence of the elements of the body and the mind , while in liberation it changes by itself within its knowledge and vision .The Jainas say that if the self were immutable, acquisition of knowledge would not be possible. Thus , before the rise of a particular knowledge , the self is devoid of it , and with the rise of that knowledge , the self is endowed with it . The self in the states of action and enjoyment is different from the self in the states of inaction and non-enjoyment .[58] From this differences , one can accept that the self can never be absolutely immutable .

From the *suddhaniscaya* point of view , the *jiva* lives with pure consciousness in the form of pure knowledge and vision which also undergo changes . From the *asudhaniscaya* point of view , the *jiva* is of the nature of impure consciousness which possesses *paryayas* or modifications under different conditions .

According to Jainism , the self or *jiva* an active agent . They do not accept the Samkhya theory of the *purusa* as passive or *udasina* . From the phenomenal point of view , the *jiva* is a doer or active agent of *karma pudgalas* or karmic matter.[59] It enjoys the fruits of its actions in the form of pleasure , pain etc. and undergoes birth and death according to its own action . The *jiva* possesses consciousness and consciousness manifests itself in the form of various mental states .These mental states are responsible for activities which produce material *karma* or *karma –pudglas* . It is , therefore , asserted that jiva is the agent of the *karma pudgalas* through mental states . However , *Pancastikayasara* describes the self as the agent of its own *bhavas* . It is not the agent of *karma pudgalas* . [60] From the noumenal point of view, *jiva* is the doer of *suddhabhavas* or pure thought and the enjoyer of its own eternal bliss . [61]

57.BDS ,3.
58.pradesasamharavisargabhyam pradipavat .TAS ,5.16.
59. Vide , *The philosophy of Jainism* , P. 89 .
60. cf. ibid.
61. cf. ibid.

Further , in the view of the Jainas , the self is endowed with movement .In its empirical state , its movement is due to the association with the *karma* matter . In its real or transcendental nature , the self is possessed of upward motion . Being , freed from the impurities of *karma* , it moves upward and reaches the end of *lokakasa* . [62]

The self in its empirical or bound state is endowed with a body which has two forms: subtle and gross. Being influenced by the *kasayas* , the self absorbs the *karmapudgalas* into the parts of its being , In the view of the Jainas , *karmapudgalas* are the subtle particles of matter . The space is full of such *karmapudgalas* and the self absorbs there *karma* particles because of *kasaya* or passion [63] *Kasaya* are four in number , viz , *krodha* (anger) *mana* (pride) *maya* (deceit) and *lobha* (greed).[64] The *karma pudgalas* and the *kasayas* are interdependent and mutually related as cause and effect from beginningless time . The *karmapudgalas* that enter into the self gather gross material elements around them . The body formed by the gross material elements is gross which is perceptible to the ordinary people . It is constituted of matter and is nourished by matter taken in the form of food etc . This body is destroyed at the time of death . The body formed by the *karmapudgalas* is the subtle body called *karmana sarira* which is imperceptible to the ordinary people .It exists with the self even after death and forms a new gross body in the next birth .This subtle body is destroyed when the self attains liberation..[65]

Both the gross and the subtle bodies are eternally changing , and the number of the parts of the bound self increases and decreases in harmony with the increase and decrease of the body . During the worldly life,the self is co-extensive with the body [66]

Again the bodies of the empirical Selves are said to be of five kinds They are : (i). *audarikam sariram* i.e. a gross body , (ii). *vaikriyam sariram* i.e. a transformation body , (iii). *aharikam sariram* i.e. a transference-body , (iv). *taijasam sariram* i.e. a fiery body and (v). *karmanam sariram* i.e. a karmic body . Of these five kinds of

62.Ibid .
63.sakasayo jivah karmabhavayogyanpudgalanadatte .Ibid ., P.75.
64.kasayah krodhadih .Ibid .,P.76.
65.Vide , *The Philosophy of Jainism* ,P.90.
66.svadehaparimanah .BDS,2.

bodies , every successive one is subtler than the preceding one . The last two types of bodies are attached to the self from beginningless time .Amongst the five kinds of bodies , *karmana sarira* is called *nirupabhoga* ,because it does not help the self in experiencing or knowing anything .But the other four bodies are called *sopabhoga* , because they help the selves in experiencing or knowing things .[67]

The Jainas hold that the relation between the body and the self is one of identify –cum-difference . They are identical because the self experiences the pains and pleasures of the body. They are different, as the self is not destroyed with the destruction of the body .From the pure point of view , the Self is not associated with anybody and senses , nor with any physical and mental qualities. In liberation, the self is completely freed from the body and the senses, and is, therefore, described as *akaya* or bodiless .[68] According to the phenomenal point of view ,sometimes a liberated self is endowed with a body a bit smaller than the body of the just preceding birth .[69]

The self is endowed with *pranas* or life powers , which are of two types : *bhavapranas* and *dravyapranas. Bhavapranas* are those which concerned with the consciousness , while those concerned with the *pudgalas* in general are called *dravyapranas* . A released *jiva* maintains only the *bhavapranas* i.e. *jnana* or knowledge , *darsana* or vision , *sukha* or happiness.[70] From the phenomenal point of view , *jiva* is also described as possessing four *dravyapranas* .They are : senses (*indriya*) energy (*bala*) , life (*auyh*) and the life power of in and out breathing (*ucchvasa*) . These four *pranas* are essential characteristics of any empirical self. [71] These four *pranas* are manifest in ten forms . The senses embraces the five sense organs . Under the life power of energy are to be understood the body (*kayah*) ,speech (*vak*) and the mind (*manah*) . Life and the life power of in and out breathing are one

67. Vide , *The Philosophy of Jainism* , P. 90.
68. Kalghatgi ,T.G., *Jaina View of Life* ,PP.36-37.
69.kimcidunah caramadehatah siddhah .BDS.14.
70. Vide , *ThePhilosophy of Jainism* , P. 88.
71.Ibid ., 89.

each . Of course , the number of *pranas* differs in different organisms because there are alsoorganisms with less than five sense organs .The most perfectly developed selves have all the ten *pranas* and the lowest have only four *pranas* .[72]

3.THE PARYAYAS OF THE SELF :

The paryayas or modifications are of five kinds , viz , (i) *aupasamika* –when the *karma –paramanus* that have entered the body of the self are suppressed and are not allowed to take any more transformation , (ii) *ksayika* –when the *karma – paramanus* are totally expeled from the body of the self .(iii) *ksayopasamika* - when the *karma –paramanus* are partly made ineffective and are partly expeled .(iv) *audayika*- when the *karma –paramanus* arise and start giving fruits ,and (v) *parninamika* –when the self does not depend upan *karman* , and remains in its own nature .[73] Of them the first four states are *naimittikas* i.e. conditioned by *karman* , while the last one is natural to consciousness .Again , the last state has three varities ,viz-*bhavyatva* , *abhavyatva* and jivatva .*Bhavyatva* is the state of that self which has the capacity to acquire the three *ratnas* ; such as –s*amyak-jnana* or proper knowledge , s*amyak-darsana* or proper faith and s*amyak-caritra* or proper behaviour *Abhavyatva* is the state of that self which does not have the capacity to acquire these three *ratnas* .*Jivatva* is synonymous with *caitanya* i.e. consciousness of the self . It is the *Jivatva* that is manifested as *jnana* and *darsana* .[74] Thus *jnana* and *darsana* are two resultants of *caitanya* and *jivatva* .

4.SIZE OF THE SELF OR JIVA :

Some philosophers like the Naiyayikas , the Vaisesikas , the Samkhyists , the Yogists , the Mimamsakas and the Advaita Vedantins regard the Self as *vibhu* or all pervasive . While the others particularly the Vaisnava Vedantins like Ramanuju , Nimbarka , Vallabha , Madhva and SriCaitanya regard it as *anuparimana* or atomic

72.Ibid .
73.aupasamikakasayikau bhavau misrasca jivasya svatatvamaudayikaparinamikau ca .SDS ,P.68.
74.jivabhavyabhavyatvadini ca .TAS, 2.7.

in size .On the other hand , the Jainas hold that the self is neither *vibhu* or all pervasive nor *anuparimana* or atomic , but *madhyamparimana* or intermediary in size . It assumes the magnitude of the body in which it resides .[75] Mallisena argues that the self cannot be regarded as all-pervasive ,because its qualities are not perceived everywhere .[76] Prabhacandra also argues that the self can not be the locus of pervasive measure like *akasa* nor of atomic measure like *paramanu ,* because it is conscious .[77] If the self were all-pervasive , it could not be contained by the small body . Further , such a self would come in contract with all the objects of the world , and as a result every *jiva* could know everything .On the other hand , if the self were atomic in size , it would not fill up the whole body .

Now this position of the Jainas raise of some problems for them .The Jainas are the believes of the theory of rebirth and uphold that the self takes rebirth after its death .In that case the problem will be when a self of a body size takes rebirth in another body , the former self may be fit in the latter body .In reply the Jainas say that although it is not of any definite size , yet , it is subject to change due to changing circumstances .It is manifested that the self contracts and expands according to the size of the body in which it is incorporated for the time being .The self is capable of adjusting the size to the physical body .as the light of the lamp placed in a large or small room illuminates the whole space of the room .Accordingly , the self is co-existence with the body .

The Jainas argue that if the self were all pervasive , it would come in contract with all the bodies , the senses and the minds simultaneously , just as the all pervasive *akasa* comes in contact with all the objects like pitchers , clothes etc , therefore , the difference of knowledge , action birth , death etc. found in different individuals could not be accounted for .[78] Thus the Jainas conclude

75.svadehaparimanah .BDS ,2.
76.atma sarvagato na bhavati sarvatra tadgunanupalabdheh.Hemacandra's comt. On
   SM ,9.
77.atma' nuparamamahattvaparimananadhikaranah -----------------iti .PKM , P.571.
78.cf *Reals in the Jaina Metaphysics* ,P.281.

that the Self is to be regarded as intermediary in size and as co existensive with the body which it occupies during its mundane existence .

5.NUMBER OF THE SELVES OR JIVAS :

According to the Jainas , there are many selvess , since it is different in every individual .[79]However , in some works of Jainism , the *jiva* is said to be one . In the *Sthanangasutra* , the Self is described as one If the selves were one , then "there would not be *sukha, dukha , bandha , moksa* etc.[80] But the oneness of the *jiva* is not acceptable to the Jainas . Hence the above view has been explained by some to mean that all the selves are of the same nature i.e. ekavidhah atmanah .In *Samayasara* , however Kundakundacarya describes the absolute oneness of the self on the strength of self realization .[81] This does not mean that the self is one of the Vedantic sense of term .It does not go against the plurality of the self.It only emphasizes the essential identity of the self .In all the *jivas* the individual characteristics are essentially the same . Thus , according to Jainism , the selves are many and different from one another .

Of course , the *jivas* are many only quantitatively , while qualitatively they are said to be all alike . The Jainas do not accept the Sankara theory of one self nor they agree with Madhva who maintains qualitative difference among the selves .

6.CLASSIFICATIONS OF THE JIVA :

In the view of the Jainas , the *jivas* are mainly divided into two types , viz , *mukta* or liberated and s*amsari* or bound . The s*amsari*-jivas are subject to birth , change and death . The *mukta-jivas* are those who are free from the cycle of birth and death , and from the resulting joys and sorrows .

The s*amsari-jivas* are further divided into *trasa* or mobile and *sthavara* or immobile . The *trasa* or mobile selves are again classified as those who have two senses , e.g. worms ; three senses , e.g. ants ; four senses ,e.g. wasps , bees etc . and

five senses , e.g. higher animals and men .The *sthavara* or immobile selves live in

---

79. atma anekah .VIP ,50.
80. Vide , *The philosophy of Jainism* , P. 95.
81.Ibid .

the atoms of earth , water , fire and air and in the vegetable kingdom and have only one senses that of touch .[82]

The liberated *jivas* are of two kinds : completely liberated (*nirvanaprapta* or *siddha*) and liberated in worldly existence (*jagatikamukta*). The *nirvanaprapta jivas* are of two types , (i). *tirthamkara-siddhas* and (ii). *Samanya-siddhas* .The *Jagotikamukta jivas* are also of two types , (i).yogins or *arhats* and (ii) *ayogins* .The *ayogins* are also of three types , (i). *acaryas* , (ii). *upadhyaya* and (iii). *saddhus* . These five kinds if liberated *jivas* i.e. *siddha* , *arhat* , *acarya* , *upadhyaya* and *saddhu* are called *panca-paramesthins*.[83]

The Jainas hold that the *mukta jiva* acquires pure , perfect and infinite knowledge revealing everything of the world . This knowledge is called *kevalajnana* .This *kevalajnana* is generally attained by the selves in their disembodied state . But one can attain it even in the embodied state who can fully develop his intrinsic nature during worldly life through rigorous practices And persons who can acquire such type of knowledge during their embodied state are called *arhatas* or *tirthamkaras*

7. PROOFS FOR THE EXISTENCE OF THE SELF OR JIVA :

The existence of the self is a pre –supposition in the Jaina philosophy , and hence , no proof is felt necessary to establish the existence of the Self . If , however , it is required to prove the existence of the self , it can be done by perception , inference and verbal testimony .[84] Mahavira says "oh Gautama , the self is *pratyaksa* , for that in which your knowledge consists is itself soul." That means the self is known in realization of 'I ' or *ahampratyaksa* , which is associated with the functions pertaining to all the three points of time.[85] The existence of the self is directly proved by such uncontradicted immediate experience as "I feel pleasure" . When we perceive the quality of a substance , we perceive the substance . For example , on seeing a rosy colour we hold that we perceive the substabnce rose to which the colour belongs.

82.tatra jiva dvividhah samsarino muktasca ------------sparsanaikendriyah .SDS ,P.70.
83. Vide , *The philosophy of Jainism* , P. 96.
84. Ibid .,P.82.
85. Ibid .

On the similar ground we can hold that the self is directly perceived , because we immediately perceive such characters of the self as pleasure , pain , remembrance , volition doubts , knowledge etc. The existence of the self may also be indirectly proved by inference . The body can be moved and controlled at will like a car , and , therefore , there must be some one that moves and controls it . The senses of sight , hearing etc. are only instruments and there must be some agent who employs them . Again , there must be some efficient cause of the body , because material objects which have a beginning are found to require agent for shaping their material cause . Thus indifferent ways the existence of the self can also be inferred .The sayings of the *Tirthankaras* also may be referred to as proofs for the existence of the self .Mahavira says "It is my word ,O Gautyama."[86]

86. Ibid .

CHAPTER –IV

CONCEPT OF LIBERATION OR MOKSA

The ultimate aim of all the systems of Indian philosophy is to show us the means for the attainment of *moksa* or liberation. Only the Carvakas do not believe in it. Brhaspati regards dependence as bondage and independence as release. All other systems accept *moksa* as the ultimate aim or *paramapurusatha* of human existence.

1.JAINA VIEW OF BONDAGE :

In Indian philosophy, bondage means in general , the cycle of birth and death and the consequent sufferings . This general conception of bondage is differently interpreted by the different systems in the light of their ideas of the individual and the world. According to the Jainas the self is inherently perfect. It has infinite potentiality within. Infinite knowledge, infinite faith, infinite power and infinite bliss are its essential qualities. There can all be realized by the self, if it can only remove from within itself all obstacles that stand in the way .Just as the sun shines forth to illuminate the entire world as soon as the atmosphere is freed of cloud and foy , similarly the self attains omniscience as soon as the obstacles are removed .It has already been mentioned that the activity of the self and *kasayas* like anger etc are the causes of bondage . *Karmans* are infra-atomic particles of matter (*pudgala*) which are produced by passions and actions of mind , body and speech moved by desire , aversion and delusion .The Jainas maintain that there are two types of *karmans* , viz. , destructive or *ghatiya karman* and non-destructive or *aghatiya karman* . The destructive *karman* are four in number .They are : (i). knowledge –obscuring action (*jnanavaraniya*) (ii). Vision –obscuring action (*darsanavaraniya*) (iii).Obstructive action (*antaraya*) and (iv).Deluding action (*mohaniya*) .The non-destructive karmans are also four .They are –(i).age-determining action (*ayus*) (ii).character -determining action (*nama*) (iii).family -determining action (*gotra*) and (iv).feeling -determining action (*vedaniya*) .Therefore , there are eight types of *karmans* in total .

1. *Jnanavaraniya* : It obscures right-knowledge and the natural omniscience of the Self , and produces degrees of knowledge and ignorance .

2. *Darsanavaraniya* : It obscures right –vision.

3. *Antaraya* : It obstructs the inborn energy of the self and prevents it from doing good actions .

4. *Mohaniya* : It deludes right vision and produces doubt , error etc.

5.*Ayus* : It determines the longevity of the self and breaks up the immortal existence into short and long individual lives.

6.*Nama* : It produces the circumstances or conditions like the body and other facilities which are necessary for the embodiement of the bodiless self .

7.*Gotra* : It determines the racial , social and geneological status of the embodied self.

8.*Vedaniya* : It obstructs the innate bliss of the self and produces emotions and feelings of pleasure , pain etc.[2]

2.*ASRAVA* :

As the nature and number of material particles attracted by the self depend on its *karman* , these particles themselves come to be called *karma*-matter or even simply *karman* .The flow of such *karma-matter* into the self is called influx (*asrava*) of *karman* .[3] When the influx of *karman* is checked and the *karma*-particles already entered into the body of the self are washed out , the self regains its real nature , and attains liberation from the worldly life .

Influx is the effect of bodily , verbal and mental actions , and thecause of the self's bondage [4] It is said to be the channel through which *karma*-matter enters into the self .It is the cause of virtue or vice .There are two kinds of influx (i). subjective influx (bhavasrava) and (ii). objective influx (dravyasrava) . The modifications of the self which generates the influx of *karma*-matter into the self is subjective influx .

2. SDS , PP , 76-77 .

3.audarikadikayadicalanadvarenatmanascalanam
yagapadavedaniyamasravah . SDS .PP . 73-74

4. asravabhedaprabhedajatam kayavanmanah / karmayogah SDS , P. 74

Subjective influx is the modification of the self through the five senses , and consists in thought –activities .It causes the physical influx of *karma-matter* into the self [5] Accordingly it is expected that the former should precede the latter , but in reality , they occur simultaneously . They are , however , said to be successive , only from the logical point of view .

Subjective influxes are of five kinds : (i).false belief , (ii).want of control .(iii). inadvertence .(iv). bodily , verbal and mental activities , and (v).passions .Objective or physical influxes are actual influxes of eight kinds *karma*-matter into the soul.

Asrava leads the self to *bandha* or bondage . As a result of *asrava* or the activity of the self , *karma*-particles enter into the self .And the Self affected by passions like , love , anger etc. absorbs these *karma*-particles into its innumerable parts ,just as a heated iron-ball absorbs the particles of water , or just as a wet cloth absorbs the dusts brought by the wind. This absorption of the *karma*-patricles by the self within itself is called *bandha* or bondage .[6] As a result of the absorption of the *karma*-matter , the self , which is intrinsically pure and perfect , becomes impure and imperfect , forgets its real nature , and undergoes the cycle of birth and death .In this state , the self's four infinite capabilities of consciousness , vision , power and bliss are obstructed by *karma*-matter and are manifested in an imperfect and limited way.

3. CAUSE OF BONDAGE .

The Jainas enumerate five cause of bondage . These are : (i).*mithyatva* or *avidya* i.e. perversity or nescience ,(ii). *avirati* i.e. non-restraint (or attachment to the worldly things like food , lodging , wealth, women etc.) (iii).*pramada* or delusion (iv). *kasaya* or passion (of anger , pride , deceit and greed) and (v). *yoga* or the activity of the self .[7] *Mithyatva* or *avidya* otherwise called *mithyadrsti* ; *darsana-moha* or *moha* , is the root cause of bondage .From *mithyatva* arises *avirati* , from *avirati* arises *pramada* ; from *pramada* arises *kasaya* ; and from *kasaya* arises *yoga* .

5. Vide , *Outlines of Indian Philosophy* , P .147 .
6. sakasayatvajjivah karmabhavayogyanpudgalanadatte   sabandhah .TAS, 8.2 .
7. mithyadarsanaviratipramadakasaya-yogabandhahetavah . TAS ,8.1.

Avidya means nescience or false notions about the self and its relation to other things .It takes the form of 'I' and 'mine' .*Avidya* or *mithyatva* has three factors-perversive view (*mithya-darsana*), perversive knowledge (*mithya-jnana*) and pervasive conduct (*mithya-caritra*) .Bondage is caused not only be perverted knowledge , but also by perverted attitude and perverted conduct .That is why , even after the attainment of right knowledge , the self remains embodied because of the operation of *karma*-matter.[8]

The bondage of the self is i.e. the self's relation with the *karma*-particles has no beginning in time .For *avidya* , the root cause of bondage is without any beginning .*Avidya* is called *darsana-moha* or delusion of vision also , which is a variety of *karman* attached to the self .That means , the root cause of bondage may be said to be *karman* also .[9]

The next cause of bondage is *avirati* .[10] It is of five kinds : (i).*himsa* or injury , (ii). *anrta* or falsehood , (iii).*caurya* or stealing (iv).*abrahmacarya* or incontinence and (v). *parigraha* or attachment towards a thing .

The third cause of bondage is pramada.[11] It is of eight kinds (i).*irsya* (ii).*bhasa* , (iii).*esana* , (iv).*adana* (v).*utsarga* (vi).*vaka* (vii).*mano* (viii).*kaya* .

The fourth cause of bondage is *kasaya* . It is of four verities (i).anger (ii).pride , (iii).deceit and (iv).greed.[12]

The fith cause of bondage is yoga . Yoga consists of the activities of mind ,Speech and body [13] Hence , this is of three kinds .

Bondage is of two kinds (i).*bhava-bandha* or subjective bondage and (ii). *dravya- bandha* or objective bondage . *Bhava-bandha* means the psychical states because of which the self comes in contact with *karma*-matter and becomes bound .These psychical states are attachment ,aversion , delusion ,anger ,pride and greed .

---

8. Lad, A .K *The Concept of Liberation in India Philosophy* ,P.39.
9.A .chakravorti's commentary on PKS, 148.
10.prthivyadisatkopadanam   sadindriyasamyamanam   caviratih .SDS, P.76.
11.pancasamititriguptisvamutsahah   pramadah .Ibid .
12.kasayah   krodhadih .Ibid .
13.kayavanmanah   karmayogah .Ibid ., P.74.

Dravya- bandha or objective bondage means the actual contact between the Self and the *karma*-matter because of which the self actually comes under the grip of bondage.[14]

Objective bondage is of two kinds , bondage of the self to good *karmans* , and its bondage to bad *karmans* .It is four kinds according to the nature (*prakrti*) of *karma* , duration (*sthiti*) of bondage , intensity (*anubhava*) and number (*pradesa*) of *karma* particles interpenetrating the self .[15] Different kinds of *karmans* determine the nature of bondage . The *karma*-matter is combined with the self for a longer or shorter duration . It may be mild or strong so that its fruition is mild or strong , immediate or delayed .The particles of *karma* –matter may be few or many , and interpenetrate the self to a small or great extent .These are the four kinds of actual bondage .The nature and extent of bondage are due to the activities of mind ,speech and body .The duration and intensity of bondage are due to emotions and passions .Passions are the internal cause of bondage .Activities of mind , speech and body are the external cause of bondage .[16]

4.SAMVARA:

It is seen in the foregoing discussion that *asrava* causes bondage of the self . *Asrava* is the ingress of *karma*-matter into the self. But ultimate aim of life is the attainment of liberation , liberation cannot be attained so long as the *karma*-matter exists in the self .Accordingly , for the attainment of liberation , it is necessary to stop the influx of *karma*-matter into the self .This stoppage of the influx of the *karma*-matter is called *Samvara* .[17] The aim of *Samvara* is to free the self from the mental defects and thereby to stop the subsequent influx of *karma*-particles .

Samvara is of two kinds (i). *bhava- samvara* or subjective inhibition and (ii).*dravya- samvara* or objective inhibition . For checking the influx of *karma* matter

---

14.Vide , *The Philosophy of Jainism* , PP,63-64.
15.ybandhascaturvidha ityuktam prakrtisthityanubhavapradesastadvidhayah .SDS ,P.76.
16. Vide , *Outlines of Indian Philosophy* , P .149 .
17.asravanirodhah samvarah . SDS ,P.78.

into the self , first it is necessary to check the modifications of the self in the form of attachment , hatred and delusion . This checking of the modifications of the self is called *bhava- samvara* .It is of two kinds : (i). *bhava-punya- samvara* or the stoppage of the modifications of the self due to auspicious mental activities and (ii). *bhava-papa- samvara* or the stoppage of the modifications of the self due to inauspicious mental activities . *Dravya- Samvara* is the checking of the actual inflow of *karma*-particles into the self through the channel of *asrava* .This inflow of *karma*-particles is stopped when the mental modifications i.e auspicious and inauspicious are stopped . Thus , *bhava- Samvara* is the cause of *dravya- samvara* .[18]

There are sixtytwo ways of *bhava- samvara* , which can bring about *dravya-samvara* or the stoppage of the actual inflow of *karma*-matter . The first five ways of stopping the inflow of *karma*-matter refer to the outward behavior , and these are called s*amitis*. These are (i).*irya-samiti* or observance of the rules of walking , (ii).*bhasa-samiti* or observance of the rules of speech, (iii). *esana- samiti* or observance of the conduct of the begging, (iv). *adanani-ksepana- samiti* or observance of the rules of keeping some portion of the alms for the performance of religious duties , and (v).utsarga or *pratisthapanasamiti* or the observance of the rules of taking and refusing or alms .[19]

Like the s*amitis*, there are rules for controlling of mind , body and speech . The conduct of controlling these three is called *gupti* or restraint .It is of three kinds – (i).*kaya-gupti* or bodily restraint , (ii). *mano-gupti* or mental restraint and (iii).*vag-gupti* or speech restraint .[20]

There are again five types of vows (*vrata*) which are to be observed . These are : (i)*ahimsa* or abstinence from injury , (ii). *anrta* or truthfulness , *(iii).asteya* or abstinence from stealing , *(iv).brahmacarya* or abstinence from sexual pleasure and (v).*aparigraha* or abstinence from owing worldly objects .[21]

18.cetanaparinamo yah karmanah asravanirodhane hetuh *I*
  sah bhavasamvarah khalu dravyasravanirodhane anyah *II* BDS ,34.
19.iryabhasaisanadananiksepotsargah samitayah . TAS ,9.5; SDS ,P.25.
20.samyag yoganigraho guptih . TAS , 9.4.
21.himsanrta-asteya-brahma-aparigrahebhyo viratir vratam .Ibid .,7.1.

One should also observe ten kinds of dharma for checking of the influx of *karma pudgalas*. These are : (i).*uttama-ksama* or excellent forgiveness , (ii). *uttama – mardava* or excellent humility ,(iii). *uttama -arjava* or excellent uprightness, (iv). *uttama satya* or excellent truth (v). *uttama sauca* or excellent cleanliness ,(vi). *uttama samyama* or excellent restraint , (vii). *uttama tapas* or excellent penance (viii). *uttama tyaga* or excellent renunciation , (ix). *uttama akincanya* or excellent indifference , and (x). *uttama brahmacarya* or excellent sex-control.[22]

Moreover , the inflow of *karma*-matter can be checked by keeping the twelve kinds of *anupreksa* i.e. disposition . Thus , one should bear in mind that (i).everything except *dharma* is transient (*anityanupreksa*) , (ii).that there is no other resort except truth (*asarananupreksa*) (iii). that a person is solely and individually responsible for his own deeds (*ekatvanupreksa* (iv).that the self is distinct from the body (*angatvanupreksa*) and (v). that the body and everything related to it are impure (*asucitvanupreksa*).Also one should contemplate (vi). about the influx of *karman* (*asravanupreksa*) ; (vii). about the cycle of birth and death (*samsaranupreksa*) ; (viii). about the checking the influx of *karman* (*samvaranupreksa*),(ix).about the removal of the *karma* –matter that has already extered into the self (*nirjaranupreksa*), (x). about the self , the body and substances of the world (*lokanupreksa*) ,(xi). about the difficulty of attaining perfect faith , perfect knowledge and perfect conduct (*bodhidurlabharupreksa*), and (xii). about the essential principles of the universe (*dharmanupreksa*)[23]

Samvara can be achieved with great difficulties and in order to be successful in that attempt one has to follow *parisaha* i.e. to undergo hardships for having control over them . The Jainas refer to twentytwo kinds of hardships . They are : (i). hunger(ii). thirst (iii). cold, (iv). heat, (v). troubles by the mosquitoes (vi). troubles by gnast, (vii).feelings of shame arising from nakedness, (viii). the feelings of

---

22.uttama-ksama-mardavarjava-satya-sauca-samyama-tapas-tyagakincanya-brahmacar-
   yani dharmah . Ibid. ,9.6.
23. lbid.9.7.

(ii). thirst (iii). cold, (iv). heat, (v). troubles by the mosquitoes (vi). troubles by gnast, (vii).feelings of shame arising from nakedness, (viii). the feelings of dissatisfactionthrough hunger, thirst etc. (ix). emotions caused by women, (x). the feeling of tiredness from journey (xi). the desire of moving from a fixed posture in meditation (xii) . The desire to have a bed ,(xiii). The feelings of anger when insulted , (xiv). the feelings of ill-will against an enemy who comes to kill, (xv). The desire of asking for anything even in great need , (xvi). The feelings of pain caused by a disease , (xvii). The feelings of pain caused by the pricking of thorns , (xviii). The feelings of displeasure from the sight of dirtiness ,(xix). the desire to get reward and honour , (xx). The feelings of pride at one's learning , (xxi). The feelings of despair arising out of failure to obtain knowledge , and (xxii). the feelings of despair from the failure to attain something .Parisaha means control over there hardships .[24]

Lastly *samvara* also includes five kinds of *caritra* or right conduct.These are (i).*samayika-samyama* i.e. giving up all bad deeds and taking up of good deeds , such as , meditation , (ii).*chedopasthapana* i.e. repentance for all the wrong deeds in front of the preceptor , (iii). *parharavisuddhi* i.e. obtaining purity by abstaining from giving injury to the living beings , (iv). s*uksma-samparaya* i.e. taking care to destroy the subtle from of greed remaining after the control of other passions ; and (v). *yathakhyata* i.e. thinking for liberation only after the conduct of all the passions .[25]

These are different types of *bhava-samvara*.When these are successfully followed, the influx of *karma* matter into the self or *jiva* is stopped.

4.NIRJARA:

Thus by s*amvara* the influx of the *karma*-particles is stopped . But the self is not yet free of the *karma* –particles which have already entered into the self . Hence , one is required to destroy the *karma –paramanus* that have already entered the body

---

24.cf.margacyavananirjarayam parisorhavyah parisahah .TAs, 9.8-9.
25.samayikacehedopasthapanapariharavisuddhisuksmasamparayayathakhyatam iti caritram. Ibid.9.18.

of the self . This destruction of *karma* –matter is called *nirjara* or shedding .[26] Like *Samvara* , *nirjara* is also of two kinds : (i).subjective shedding or *bhava- nirjara* and (ii). objective shedding or *dravya- nirjara* . Subjective shedding is the pure modifications of the self which facilitates the separation of *karmanas* from the self. Objective shedding is their actual separation from the self .For destroying the *karmas,* which have interpenetrated the Self, one has to practice penances .Penances are of twelve types. Of them, six are external austerities and six are internal ones .

The six external austerities are : (i).*anasana* (fasting) (ii).*avamodarya* (regulation of diet by eating less than one's capacity) (iii).*vrttisamksepa* (limiting the quantity of food) (iv).*rasa-tyaga* (abstaining from enjoying any particular taste in food) (v).*kaya klesa* (torturing the body) and (vi). *samlinata* (aviodance of temptation). *Kayaklesa* can be observed by sitting in meditation in summer on heated stones in the open sun or in winter in the coldest places , by pulling out the hair by the roots , by the mortification of flesh , and so on .Avoidance of temptation is possible by controlling the senses , by controlling anger , deceit , pride , greed etc. by refraining from the exercise of the mind , body and speech , and by being very careful about the place of stay so that no woman lives near or s*amlinanta.*[27]

The six internal austerities are : (i).*prayascitta* (confession of crime and performance of austerities for its atonement) (ii).*vinaya* (reverence to the ascetics and to all who are superior in knowledge , vision and conduct) (iii).*vaiyavacca* (service to the ascetics and to the poor , helpless and sufferers , by giving food , water , shelter , clothes etc.)(iv).*svadhyaya* (study of scriptures) (v).*vyutsarga* (giving up of objects and thoughts of the mundane world) and (vi). *dhyana* (performing meditation as prescribed in the sacred scriptures). [28]

These are the means of destroying the *karma-pudgalas* which have entered into the *jiva* or self .

26.cf. arjitasya karmanastapahprabhrtibhirmirjaranam nirjarakhyam tatvam. SDS ,P.80.
27.TAS, 9.19.
28. Ibid. 9.20.

6.NATURE OF LIBERATION :

It is evident from our foregoing discussion that the bondage of the self is its association with matter. Hence , liberation must mean the complete dissociation of the self from *karma*-matter . when the *karma* –matter are completely dissociated then self attains its real nature of endless vision , endless knowledge , endless power , endless bliss and infiniteness .[29] It has already been seen that nescience , unrestraint , delusion , passions and the activity of the self are the causes of bondage . Because of the activity of the self , *karma* –particles enter into the body of the self. Then , the self affected by passions like anger , pride etc. absorbs the *karma* –particles into its innumerable parts , as a result of which its nature becomes impure .This state is called bondage .[30] Then if a person willing to attain liberation is to stop the influx of the *karma*-matter , and this stage is called s*amvara* .Then , again the *karma*-matter that has already entered into the self are to be destroyed or removed , and this destruction of *karma* –matter called *nirjara* .And when the self is thus fully freed from the *karma*-matter , it *nirjara* .And when the self is thus fully freed from the *karma*-matter , it realizes its own real nature characterized by the four infinite qualities , such as , infinite vision , infinite knowledge ,infinite power and infinite bliss .This is the stage of liberation .[31]

7.TYPES OF LIBERATION :

According to the Jainas liberation is of two types : (i). *bhava-moksa* or subjective liberation and (ii).*dravya-moksa* or objective liberation . *Bhava-moksa* is freedom from the four destructive *karmans* , viz., -*jnanavaraniya* , *darsanavarniya* , *mohaniya* and *antaraya* .when these four destructive *karmans* are destroyed , the self is endowed with omniscience or *anantajnana* and is called *kevalin.*[32] Along with this

,

29.krtsnakarmaksayo moksah. TAS ,10.3.
30.bhavanimitto bandhah bhavo ratiragadvesamohayutah . PKS ,148.
31.bandhahetvabhavanirjarabhyam krtsnakarmavipramoksanam moksah . SDS ,P.80.
32.moksaksayaj jnanadarsanavaranantarayaksayacca kevalam. TAS10.1, also BDS ,15.

the self attains endless vision , endless power , and endless bliss . The *Uttaradhyayana-sutra* says that the destruction of the *mohaniyakarmans* makes the self pure , that of the *jnanavaraniya karmans* leads to omniscience , that of the *darsanavaraniya karmanas* produces endless vision , that of the *antaraya karmans* bring forth endless power .The destruction of al these four types of *karman* gives rise to endless bliss.[33] n this stage , however , the self is nit freed from the mind , body i.e. even after the attainment of *bhava-moksa* , the worldly life continues to exist .Because in this state , the four conditions of bondage , viz. , *mithyatva , avirati , pramada* and *kasaya* are destroyed , but yoga or action , the fifth condition of bondage remains .Therefore , in this state , the elements of mind , body and speech exist , and the self has to perform actions through them .Accordingly it is not complete liberation , if the other four non-destructive *karmanas* are not destroyed .The actual separation of all *karmans* from the self is called *dravya-moksa* .In the state of *dravya–moksa* , the four non-destructive *karmans* , Viz. , *ayu , nama , gotra* and *vedaniya* are destroyed .When the self achieves *dravya-moksa* , it is freed from the worldly life and attains the state of a *siddha* or one completely freed from bondage .[34]

As soon as the self becomes free from all the *karmanas* and *bhavas* it gets a kind of impulse from its release from bondage which leads it upwards .[35] The upward motion of the liberated self is explained with the help of few examples : (i). As the potter's wheel goes on revolving even after the stoppage of the act of spinning , because of the force given to it , or (ii). as agourd covered with clay sinks down into water and goes up to the surface of water when the cover of clay is dissolved , or (iii).as the flame of a lamp naturally goes upward .[36] In this way , the self also goes upward when it is freed from all the *karma*-matter . It is held by the Jainas that this

33. Vide , *The Philosophy of Jainism* , PP,126.
34. Ibid. P.125.
35.tadanantaramurdhvam gacchatyalokantat . SDS , P.80.
36. Ibid., P.81.

upward movement of the self is natural to the self .During bondage , this capability remains suppressed and in liberation it reappears .And when this natural capability reappears there is nothing to hinder it from its moving upwards .[37]

Thus going upwards , the liberated self reaches a place lying at the top of the heaven called s*avarthasiddhi* . This place is called s*iddhasita* which exists at the *lokagra* or the extreme end of *lokakasa* i.e. at the juncture between *lokakasa* , the mundane space and *alokakasa* , the transcendental space . It is an eternal land full of pure bliss and free from age , disease , birth , death , fear and misery . The self which has attained complete liberation attains this land , resides there forever , and never comes back to the world of misery . Being freed from *karman* , the liberated self does not move into the *lokakasa* , nor does it enter into the *alokakasa* , for there is no principle of motion .[38]

According to some philosophers , *bhava-moksa* accepted by the Jainas is identical with *jivanmukti* or "liberation during life ", accepted by the Advaita Vedantins . There are again some thinkers who hold that the Jainas do not accept *jivanmukti* or liberation during bodily existence . It is argued that according to the Jainas *mukti* means complete dissociation from *karmans* including the age determining *karmas* .And as the dissociation from the age- determining *karmans* is necessarily and immediately followed by the destruction of the body , there can not be any *jivanmukti* . But as a matter of fact *bhavamoksa* which consists in the destruction of the four destructive *karmans* is also a form of moksa . It corresponds to the *jivanmukti* of the Advaita-vedantins .Therefore , we may say that *jivanmukti* is accepted in Jainism also.

8.NATURE AND QUALITIES OF THE LIBERATED SELF :

Nemicandra holds that the liberated self also possesses a form which is a bit smaller than the body occupied by it immediately before its liberation [39] On the other hand Acaranga-sutra maintains that a liberated self is not long , not short , not

37. Ibid., P.80.
38.dharmastikayabhavat . TAS, 10.8.
39.kimcidunah caramadehatah siddhah . BDS ,14.

circular not quadrangular , not expanded , not male , not female and not eunuch , and that it has no form , no colour , no smells , no touch etc.[40] Thus , it appears that the Jainas uphold completely opposite views regarding the question whether the liberated self possess a body or not . However , this difference of view results from the difference of viewpoint . From the transcendental point of view (*Niscaya-naya*) the self is devoid of any form .But from the empirical point of view the self is said to possess a form a bit smaller than the body of its immediately preceding birth. K.P. Sinha opines that " If therefore seems that the self is said to have a form only for maintaining an identity between the self liberated self and its pre-liberation birth ."[41]

The liberated self realizes its four infinite qualities which are intrinsic to its very nature .The liberated Self is omniscient , all the objects of the world being revealed to it , and is endowed with immeasurable power.Further , the liberated self enters into the ocean of bliss and enjoys immeasurable and incomparable bliss which is not disturbed by any element.[42]The liberated self is free from *karma*-matter , birth , disease , old age and death and also from fear and misery . A liberated self does not became bound again , since liberation is indestructible and eternal .Just as a car can not move when its wheels are destroyed , so a liberated *jiva* does not undergo birth , death etc. as its acts are destroyed .[43] Nemicandra says that the liberated self is endowed with eight qualities , such as , perfectness or *samyaktva , knowledge* or *jnana* , vision or *darsana* , prowess or *virya* , fineness or *suksmatva* , capability to enter anywhere or *avagahana* , freedom from heaviness and lightness or *agurulaghu* and unobstructedness or *avyabadha* .[44]

9.PATH OF LIBERATION:

For attaining this type of liberation the Jainas prescribe three means which are together called *ratnatraya* . The three jewels or *ratnatraya* are : right faith (*samyak-*

40.AS, 1.56,PP.153-154.
41.Sinha , K.P. *The Philosophy of Jainism* ,P.128.
42. Vide , *The Philosophy of Jainism* , P,129.
43. Ibid.
44. Ibid.

darsana) , right knowledge (*samyak-jnana*) and right conduct (*samyak –caritra*) .According to the Jainas , all these three means are essential , none of them taken independently can bring forth liberation .In the *Tattvarthadhigama sutra* , Umasvati says that , the path of liberation lies through right faith , knowledge and conduct .Liberation is the joint effect of these three .[45] So a person desiring to attain liberation should cultivate all these three means of faith , knowledge and conduct , just as a patient must have faith in the doctor's prescription , know the medicine prescribed and actually take the medicine . The Jainas do not believe that liberation can be attained by divine grace .In their view , man is the architect of his own fate ; he can attain liberation only by his own effort .

a.SAMYAK DARSANA :

Samyak-darsana or right faith is sincere belief in the essential principles of Jainism , viz. *jiva ,ajiva , asrava ,bandha , sam-vara ,nirjara* and *moksa* . Umasvati defines right faith as the attitude of respect (*sraddha*) towards truth . This faith may be inborn and spontaneous in some ,in others it may be acquired by learning or culture .In any case , faith can arise only when the *karmans* that stand in its way i.e. the tendencies that cause disbelief are worn out .

Samyak –darsana or right faith is the starting point of spiritual life .It essentially precedes right knowledge , for without a right faith , right knowledge can not be attained .Right faith is of two types , such as , natural and learnt .The first arises naturally without the advices of others , while the second arises through the advices of others .[47]

b. SAMYAK JNANA :

samyak jnana or right knowledge is the knowledge of all categories accepted by the Jaina sages , viz. , the self and the others . This knowledge must be free from doubts , illusion and uncertainty .[48] Right knowledge is of great importance , since

45.samyagdarsanajnanacaritrani militani moksakaranam na pratyekam .
   yatha rasayanam----------- na pratyekam. SDS, P.66.
46. tattvartha sraddhanam samyagdarsanamiti SDS , P.62., also TAS ,1.2.
47.tannisargad adhigamad va. TAS,1.3.
48.yathavasthitatattvanam sanksepadvistarena va /
   yovavodhastamatrahuh samyagjnanam manisinah // SDS ,P.63.

when a person attains the knowledge of truth , he realizes the nature of virtue and vice and can ascertain what vows he should perform.

c SAMYAK CARITRA :

Samyak caritra or right conduct means a line of proper conduct .It is the devoid of all kinds of bad *karmans* .There are five kinds *vratas* in *samyakcaritra* , viz ,(i) *ahimsa* , (ii) *sunrta* , (iii) *asteya* , (iv) *brahmacarya* and (v) *aparigraha* [49]

According to the Jainas , a spiritual person must follow right conduct as well as right faith and right knowledge for the attainment of liberation.One devoid of right faith can not have right knowledge ; one devoid of right knowledge can not have right conduct ; and again , one devoid of right conduct can not attain liberation .

It has already been mentioned that passions attract the flow of *karma* matter into the self , Passions are due to *avidya* or nescience .So , nescience is the real cause of bondage .This nescience can be destroyed to only by right knowledge .So , right knowledge is the cause of liberation .This right knowledge is produced by right faith .So , faith is also necessary knowledge . It is only by right conduct from which we can gain right knowledge .[50] Right knowledge dawns when all the *karmans* are destroyed by right conduct .

Hence , *samyak darsana , samyakjnana* and *samyakcaritra* , all are the means of the path of liberation .

49.sarvathavadyayoganam tyagascaritramucyate *I*
   kirtitam tadhimsadivratabhedena pancadha *II*
   ahimsasunrtasteyabrahmacaryaparigrahah   *II* SDS ,P.65.
50.Vide ,*A critical survey of Indian Philosophy* ,P.66.

CHAPTER – V

CRITICISM OF THE JAINA CONCEPT OF THE SELF.

The concept of the self is advocated by the Jainas has been vehemently criticized by other philosophers .The main point of criticism these philosophers refer to the size of the self .It has already been discussed that the Jainas maintain that the self is co-existent with the body and is of the size of the body .As such, it is of a intermediary measure .This view of the Jainas has been strongly criticised by the opponents .In criticizing the Jaina theory of the self , the Vedantins and the Samkhyas have brought about a number of charges against this theory .In the following lines we are going to discuss the chief arguments of Sankara against Jainism .

1. SANKARAS CRITICISM OF JAINA VIEW OF THE SELF :

1. Refuting the view of the Jainas regarding the size of the self ,Sankara argues that if the self is of the size of the body, then it would be constituted of parts, so it can not be eternal. The Jainas also say that the self undergoes rebirth. So if a man is to be reborn as an elephant, then the self of the former body would not pervade the whole body of the latter. Again, if a man is to be born as an ant, then the body of the latter would not be wholly contained in the body of the former .The same difficulty arises with respect to the different stages like childhood, youth, old age etc. in a single individual .[1]

Now, the Jainas may hold that the self has infinite parts and these get condensed in a small body and expanded in a large one. Then, the question arises: is there any hindrance as to the different parts of the self becoming concentrated at the same place or not? If there be any obstruction, then the infinite parts will not be included in the same limited space .Again, if there be no obstruction, then all the parts will be accommodated in the place occupied by a single part .Therefore, there will be no possibility of increase in size .As a result the embodied self will be atomic in size .Besides, it can not even be imagined that the self that is limited by the size of

1. BSSB, 2.2.34.

the body should have infinite parts.[2] 2. Further, the body being *savayana* or composed of parts is subject to increase and decease. Hence, if the self is regarded as equal to the size of the body it assumes, then it will have to be regarded as increasing and deceasing. Consequently the self will become non-eternal.And if it is non-eternal and ever-changing, then bondage and liberation cannot be predicted of it.[3]

The Jaina view of bondage assumes that the self being surrounded by eight kinds of *karman* remains sunk in the sea of the world like a ground which remains sunk in the water, when smeared with clay .The self floats upward when the bond of *karman* is snapped, just like the gourd from which the clay is washed off . This is liberation according to the Jainas .Moreover; the parts that come and go will be different from the self because, they are adventitious like the bodies etc. In that case it would have to be accepted that some of the parts will be the self which is everlasting. Again a question also arises here: where from the incoming parts emerge and outgoing parts submerge? As the self is not a material, therefore,   the parts can not come out from the elements and merge into the elements. Further, in some case, the nature of the self will remain in determinate for the incoming and outgoing parts will have no definite measurement. Thus, because of such defects, it is not possible to accept a successive increase or decrease in the parts of the self.[4]

3. The Jainas also says that the size of the self at the time of release is permanent. Similarly it has to be assumed that earlier initial size and the intervening size of the self should also be permanent, so that there will be similarity among the sizes of the self. Now if it is permanent, it can not have been created, for nothing created is eternal and permanent t. If it is not created it must have existed in beginning and middle as well. In other words, the size of the self must always be the same. It may be either minute or great, and it can never be medium and minute or great, and it can never be medium and changing.[5]

2. Ibid.
3. Ibid .2.2.35.
4. Ibid.
5 Ibid .2.2.36.

However the Jainas do not conform to the view of Sankara and refute these arguments. According to them, the self is endowed with the capability of being expanded and contracted, and, hence it is possible for the self to expand or contract it to adjust itself to a particular body, big or small.[6]They also do not accept the position that things endowed with parts are necessarily non eternal. In their view, though the world is endowed with parts, yet, it is eternal. In the same way, the self also may be eternal in spite of its being endowed with parts.[7]

2 .SAMKHYA CRITICISM OF JAINA VIEW OF THE SELF:

The Samkhyists also criticized the Jaina theory of the self. In the following lines, we are going to discuss about the chief arguments of Samkhyists against Jainism:

1. The Jainas accept the rebirth of the self. But, how can it be possible for rebirth of a birthless self? The Samkhyas hold that in reality ,what undergoes rebirth is not the self but the subtle body .

The subtle body is consisted of seventeen parts , having the sense-organs , the motor-organs, the *pranas*, the *manas* and the *buddhi* as its components .[8]

The subtle body acts like a dramatic actor, on account of its connection with the causes i.e. virtue, nice etc and effects i.e. in the shape of the taking up of all different kinds of physical bodies. So, just as a dramatic actor playing different parts like Parasurama or Yudhisthira , the subtle body also occupying different kinds of physical bodies , act like a man[9]

2. Against the Jaina view of the medium or limited size of the self, the Samkhyas argue that the self that is described as limited is not the real self but the empirical self or the subtle body (*Suksmadeha*) .[10]

---

6. Upasamharaprasarpatah .BDS, 10.
7. VTP, PP .202-203.
8. purusarthahetukamidam nimittanaimittikaprasangena *I*
   prakrtervibhutvayogannatavad vyavatisthate lingam *II* STK, under SK, 42.
9. yatha hi talastam ---------- suksmasariramityarthah . Ibid.
10. Sinha, K.P, *Reflexions on Indian Philosophy*, PP.178-179.

But the Jainas refute these arguments. The Jainas further hold that the self is endowed with the capability of being expanded and contracted , and , hence it is possible for the self to expand or contract itself to adjust itself to a particular body , big or small . They also do not accept the position that things endowed with parts are necessarily non-eternal. They already hold that the self also may be eternal in spite of its being endowed with parts. They also hold that the self is limited in its empirical state. But it is unlimited in its liberated state. They also argue against the view of the *suksmadeha* of the Samkhyas.

In their counter argument the Jainas puts the same question which was put to them by other philosophers .They ask: how, in the case of rebirth, the *suksmadeha* of a man could be contained by the body of an ant or the body of an elephant ? So, they hold that the *suksmadeha* of the Samkhya and the self of the Jainas are not made of gross elements; but they are made of fine elements and are capable of being expanded or contracted in consonance with their limiting conditions .[11]

But in some cases, the Jainas also say that the self in its real nature is not intermediary in size, but it is all-pervasive. There are the following arguments regarding this view:

1. According to the Jainas, the self is of the nature of knowledge which is limited in the state of bondage but unlimited in liberation.

2.The self is endowed with four infinite qualities , viz ; infinite knowledge , infinite vision , infinite power and infinite bliss .[12]All of which are realized by the self in liberation .This also indicates that the real self is all pervasive in measure .

3. Brahmadeva says that the self is in reality *akaya* or bodiless, *amurta* or not gross and *nirakara* or formless. The *Uttaradhyayana* sutra also describes the self as formless .[13].A thing having intermediary measure have in size . Some form or body,

---

11. Upasamharaprasarpatah .BDS, 10.
12. sarvam tato janati pasyati camohana bhavati nirantarayah *I*
   bhavatyanantasukhi krtarthah *II   Uttaradhyayana –sutra* . 32,109-110.
13. Bradmadeva's comt. On BDS, 51.

but as the self is bodiless and formless, it necessarily means that the self is not limited in size.

4.Further , the *Acarangasutra* says that the liberated self is not long nor short , not round , nor atomic , not extended and soon .[14] This also indicates that the self in its real nature is of unlimited size.

From all these arguments it can be said that according to the Jainas also, the real self is all-pervasive in measure .It is only the Empirical self which is limited in size.

14.Acarangasutra ,1.56.

CHAPTER – VI

CONCLUDING REMARKS

From our foregoing discussion it is evident that Jainism is one of the most important heterodox philosophical systems of India . It occupies a unique place in the philosophical   of India , ray   of the   world Its theories of *Anekantavada* and *Syadvada* give it a distinct status among other systems of philosophy .

According to the Indian theory of *anekantavada* nothing can be said to be possessing a character or characters absolutely. From different point of view, a thing can be described as having different or even opposite characters. Jaina concept of the self is also explained from this standpoint of *anekantavada.*

Among all the heterodox systems of Indian philosophy only the Jainas admit the reality of a permanent self as a knowing , feeling and active agent .In fact there are two realities found in the Jaina philosophy, viz., self and the not self (*ajiva*) .The Jainas hold that the , which eternal spiritual substance, incorporeal and immaterial. It is also the knower, enjoyer and active agent. The Jainas admit that the most important quality of the self is consciousness. This consciousness has two manifestations, namely, vision and knowledge, which are jointly called *upayoga.* And this *upayoga* is the essential character of the self. They also hold that the self is naturally pure, free, perfect and divine, and endowed with *anantacatustaya* (four infinities). These are infinite knowledge, infinite bliss and infinite power. When the self is free from all kinds of *karma* particles, then he attains liberation.

The Jaina doctrine of *karman*, which is regarded by them as the root cause of bondage of the self is distinct from other systems. In their view, *karman* is material; *karmans* are the subtle particles of matter called *pudgalas*. These karma-particles penetrate into the self and get intermixed with the self. The absorption of karma particles by the self is bondage in Jaina philosophy. The Jainas admit that there are three means for attaining liberation. These are, right faith, right knowledge and right conduct.

Regarding the size of the self also the Jainas differ from other philosophers. They admit that the self is neither *vibhu* nor *anu* in measure, but *madhyamaparimana*. The Jaina view of this medium size of the *jiva* has come under strong attack from the Advaita Vedantins and Samkhya philosophers. It is true that some Jainas have accepted that the real self is all pervasive. But it can be assumed that is a later development; it is not the general view of the Jainas. The Jainas may have accepted this view only being attacked by the opponents.

In this way we find that the Jaina concept of the self is distinct in many ways from other philosophical sects. Jainsm holds a unique position in Indian philosophy with its material *karman*, intermediary dimension of the self and the theory of *anekantavada*.

ABOUT AUTHOR

Ms. Deepa Baruah was born in Nagaon district of Assam. She completed her H.S.L.C. Examination in the year of 2000. She became graduate in the year of 2005 from Nagaon College with Major subject in Sanskrit. She took master degree from Gauhati University in the year of 2007 in Sanskrit with specialization in philosophy. She has done her M. Phill Degree from Gauhati University in the year of 2009. She has done her M.Phill on the subject entitled "A Critical Study of the Jaina Concept of Self" based on Jaina Philosophy.

She has been serving as a teacher in Chinmoya Mahavidyalaya from 2009 to 2010 on a temporary basis.

Now she is a research scholar under Gauhati university.

www.ingramcontent.com/pod-product-compliance
Lightning Source LLC
Chambersburg PA
CBHW060412050426
42449CB00009B/1954